DVOŘÁK

Klänge aus Mähren.

13 DUETTE

für

Sopran und Alt

mit Begleitung des Pianoforte

von

ANTON DVOŘÁK.

Der Text nach mährischen Nationalliedern übersetzt
von J. S. DEBRNOV.

→ Op. 32. ←

Ent.ᵈ Stat. Hall.

Verlag und Eigenthum
von
N. SIMROCK in BERLIN.

1878.
Lith. Anst. v. C.G.Röder Leipzig.

Frontispiece: Title page of the first edition of the Moravian Duets,
the first Dvořák composition which Simrock published

DVOŘÁK
Hans-Hubert Schönzeler

Marion Boyars

London · New York

First published in Great Britain and the United States in 1984 by
MARION BOYARS PUBLISHERS
18 Brewer Street, London W1R 4AS. and
262 West 22nd. Street, New York, N.Y. 10011.

Distributed in the United States by
The Scribner Book Companies Inc.

Distributed in Australia by
Thomas C. Lothian Pty
11 Munro Street, Port Melbourne, 3207.

Distributed in Canada by
John Wiley & Sons Canada Ltd.

British Library Cataloguing in Publication Data
Schönzeler, Hans-Hubert
  Dvořák.
  I. Dvořák, Antonín   2. Composers—
  Czechoslovakia—Biography
  I. Title
780′.92′4   ML410.D99

Library of Congress Cataloging in Publication Data
Schönzeler, Hans-Hubert
  Dvořák.
  "Chronological list of works": p.
  Includes index.
  Bibliography: p.
  1. Dvořák, Antonín, 1841-1904.   2. Composers—
Czechoslovakia—Biography.   I. Title
ML410.D99S345 1984   780′.92′4[B]   83-11823

ISBN 0-7145-2575-8 Cloth

Typeset in 11 point Souvenir
by Essex Photo Set, Rayleigh, Essex.

*Printed in Great Britain by Robert Hartnoll Ltd.
Bodmin, Cornwall.*

CONTENTS

Also by Hans-Hubert Schönzeler:
Bruckner
Of German Music (Editor)

To the memory of my friend, Karel Mikysa

LIST OF ILLUSTRATIONS

LIST OF ILLUSTRATIONS (cont.)

LIST OF ILLUSTRATIONS (cont.)

FOREWORD

It is fashionable nowadays to write a 'definitive' work on any given subject, but this term is rather meaningless as, in the interval which elapses between an author finishing a manuscript and the day when his book actually appears in print, new discoveries may have been made and new information come to light. This volume makes no claim to be in any way 'definitive': its main purpose is to bring the personality of the man Dvořák a little nearer to the public. Also it is hoped that it will stimulate more interest in his music, and especially that those who only know him from a handful of works such as the Humoresque and the Slavonic Dances, the 'New World' Symphony and the *Karneval* Overture, the Symphonic Variations and the Cello Concerto will be encouraged to widen the horizon of their listening to the many other beautiful and enjoyable works which stem from his pen. I have also written this book out of my own love of Bohemia, its people and its music, and in this love Dvořák takes a place in the front rank.

One of the main problems which faced me in compiling this volume was the matter of names and titles, as I did not want to complicate the style of the book unnecessarily for the English reader, and a compromise had therefore to be reached in certain respects. As far as place names are concerned, I have adhered to those which are customary in English usage where I felt this was expedient. Naturally it would be odd to speak of 'Praha' instead of Prague, and of 'Plzeň' instead of Pilsen. On the other hand, the towns of Brno or Olomouc are now generally referred to by their Czech names, and Nelahozeves is so little known that there is no need to call it 'Mühlhausen' as it was in Dvořák's day. The hardest decision to make was in the case of Karlovy Vary or Karlsbad. I opted for Carlsbad, as spelling it with a 'C' was customary in the 19th century.

The variants to be found in the names of composers, particularly those of the 18th century, are mentioned in the text. In addition, many aristocratic Czech families had a habit of writing their names sometimes in Czech, sometimes in German, such as Kaunic or Kaunitz. I have adopted the principle of using the Czech spelling when the persons in question lived in Bohemia, and the German spelling for members of the family who had made Vienna their permanent place of residence. But in most cases – as I did with the names of places – I have given the alternative version in brackets when the particular name is mentioned for the first time.

With the titles of Dvořák's compositions I have proceeded in a somewhat similar manner. Works where the title is of a generic nature such as Slavonic Dances, Moravian Duets, Legends and the like I have simply adopted the English titles. In the case of operas, overtures and similar works I have used the original Czech title whenever it is quite close to English spelling and pronunciation and cannot cause any confusion. In other cases I have used the official English names as given in the Burghauser Catalogue but, again, also giving Dvořák's Czech title at least once.

It is very difficult to learn Czech, and I doubt whether many people from the western world have mastered the intricacies of its pronunciation to perfection. It is impossible to go into all the details; suffice it to give a few general guidelines to the basic principles of Czech pronunciation:

1) In Czech, vowels are always pure, such as they are in Italian.

Consonants are pronounced much as they are in English, but it should be noted that the letter 'c' is always pronounced as a 'ts' such as in 'ca*ts*', and the 'r' is always rolled as it is in the North of England.

2) The accent in Czech *invariably* lies on the first syllable of each word, even when that first syllable consists of consonants only – such as in the name of the town of Brno ('*Br̓* no').

3) There are three accents in Czech. The first two of these merely serve to lengthen the vowel: an accent which is similar to the *accent aigu* in French (´) and the '°', the latter only ever occurring on a 'u'; but it should be noted that these accents only *lengthen* the vowels on which they appear and *never* alter the fact that the *stress* still remains on the first syllable. More difficult is the third accent, the so called 'háček' (˘). The only vowel this is used for is the 'e', thereby turning its pure sound into a 'ye'. When it appears on consonants it has a softening effect, turning a 'c' into a 'tch', an 's' into a 'sh', a 'z' into a sound as in French 'jour', and an 'n' into the same sound we find in the Spanish 'Señor'. The most difficult sound to transcribe into English is the 'r̓': it is a mixture between a rolled 'r' and a 'ž' and can perhaps be best described by the word 'surge' as pronounced by a North Countryman.

I would also like to point out that, in order not to clutter up the text and impede fluent reading, I have relegated all matters concerning the numbering of Dvořák's works to the Appendices. From these it will be seen that I am a fervent advocate of the 'Burghauser' numbering, and it went against the grain to refrain from using it in the main text of the book. However, these Burghauser numbers have not yet become a matter of common usage; many readers will still be in the habit of identifying Dvořák's compositions by their old opus numbers, and to make matters easier for them I have added these after the main mention of each work, albeit in brackets. Let us hope that, when this book goes into its second edition, the time will be ripe to substitute the Burghauser numbers throughout.

Lastly, there are many institutions and personal friends to whom I must express my sincere gratitude for their assistance: The Antonín Dvořák Museum and the Antonín Dvořák Society, Prague; The British Council, London; the Czech Embassy (London) and the Ministry of Culture of the ČSR; the Czech Music Information Centre, Prague; Editio Supraphon (Artia), Prague;
Dr. Jiří Berkovec, Arthur Boyars, Dr. Jarmil Burghauser, Dr. John Clapham, Dr. Jiřina Fikezová, Andrew Guyatt, Dr. Karel Mikysa, Kenneth L. Pearson, Harry Steinhauer.

Hans-Hubert Schönzeler
London, 1983

MUSICA BOHEMICA

Civilized man, living in a world riddled with artificiality, is in danger of forgetting primary phenomena. In our day it seems necessary to point out that melody is such a primary phenomenon, and that there has never been a period in history when melody was not the essence of what people considered to be music.

Hans Gál[1]

Different nations are endowed with different gifts. When it comes to music, Bohemia has few equals and no superiors, and to say of a Bohemian that he is musical is almost tautologous. Antonín Dvořák was one of the world's supreme melodists who can bear comparison even with that greatest melodist of all times, Franz Schubert (whose parents, incidentally, also stemmed from Moravia and Bohemian Silesia). But whereas many other composers can be dealt with *per se*, in the case of Dvořák it is of the greatest importance to trace his historic, geographic and cultural heritage in order to gain a full awareness of the essence of his music.

Musica Bohemica, Bohemian music indeed! Its songs, its dances, its folk-melodies and rhythms go back to dark and

---

[1]*Franz Schubert and the Essence of Melody* (London 1974).

distant days. The names of the early composers have sunk into oblivion, but these men constitute the fertile soil from which grew a wealth of new music – it is the soil of that basin, roughly rectangular in shape, which lies at the very centre of Europe, with ranges of low, wooded mountains forming natural boundaries in the North, West and South. This is the Bohemia and Moravia, now known as the Czech Lands, whose heart is Prague. Due to its central position, Bohemia (let us use this general term for the entire area) enjoyed advantages and disadvantages, for it always has been and still is at the crossroads: here the trading route from East to West crosses with that from South to North; here East meets West. Gallic tribes settled in this area in about 500 B.C.; they seem to have stayed for over four hundred years and, according to latest discoveries, appear to have had contact with Greek civilization. One of these Gallic tribes were the Boii, and it is presumably to them that Bohemia owes its name.

In the last century B.C. Germanic tribes took over, and in the first four centuries A.D. the area suffered wave after wave of invaders during the mass shift of population in Europe, culminating in the invasion of the Huns and Avars. It was only towards the second half of the 6th century that Slavonic tribes came to Bohemia, the main one being the 'Czechs', so named after their legendary chieftain Čech, and in the 7th century Samo's Bohemian Kingdom became the first western Slavonic state. It was eventually succeeded by the Moravian Empire in the 9th century at about the same time that the area was christianized from Constantinople, and these events again coincided with the foundation of Prague Castle. With the Přemyslide dynasty which, according to legend, began with Queen Libuše who also founded the first castle at Vyšehrad and the city of Prague, the centre of gravity shifted from Moravia to Bohemia.

The ascent to greatness began under Václav (921-29), Saint and King of Bohemia – and familiar to all English-speaking people as the 'Good King Wenceslas' of the Christmas carol. Prague became a bishopric in 973, and as early as 965 the

Arabian merchant Ibrahim Ibn Jakub, writing about his travels, describes Prague as a 'wealthy mercantile town'. The Přemyslide dynasty – the only indigenous dynasty which Bohemia ever had – came to an end in about 1300, to be succeeded after a short while by Jan of Luxemburg (1310-46) and then that greatest of all Bohemian kings, the only Czech ever to become Emperor of the Holy Roman Empire: Charles IV (1346-78). This was the longest span in its history that Bohemia was a strong, independent and forward-looking country, the only period during which it was not subjected to continuous wars, invasions, domination and oppression. It is rightly called the Golden Age, for during that time, out of all the various influences and elements, the Czech people forged their own national character, a character which they have proudly preserved ever since, at times against the most overwhelming odds. Under Charles IV, who combined nationalism (in its best sense) with patronage of the Arts and Sciences, Prague became the Golden Prague and the City of the Hundred Spires. Not only did Charles IV adorn his city and his country with castles and beautiful buildings, not only did he found in Prague in 1348 the oldest university in central Europe, but he also encouraged music on a lavish scale, and the polyphony of his Bohemia can have had little to surpass it, by all accounts, in the rest of the world.

As is inevitable owing to the lack of a musical notation, relatively little is known about Bohemian music in those early days, although it is reasonably certain that there always has been a strong vocal tradition, both secular and sacred. The oldest Bohemian melody we know is the *Hospodine, pomiluj ny* ('Lord, have mercy on us') which, according to tradition, was composed in 972 by Bishop Adalbert of Prague, later canonized as Sv. Vojtěch. Of course it was handed down orally – the earliest manuscript sources date from the 14th century – and it is a chant which has been venerated by the Czech people throughout the ages as has the Hymn of Sv. Václav which probably dates from the 11th century. Naturally Prague and its Cathedral of St. Vitus (*Sv. Vít*) became a centre of music as far back as the 11th century, and one of the first musicians to emerge from the shrouds of anonymity is Záviš (1379-1418), head of the Music School at the University, whom Rosa Newmarch describes as the 'Bohemian Tallis'. That sacred polyphonic music was flourishing during this Golden Age has already been mentioned, but at Court and in the palaces of the nobility there must also have been much music-making, and it is interesting to note from contemporary reports that even in those days there was a predominance of music for wind instruments – a predominance which has remained a characteristic of Bohemian music right up to the 19th century.

With the death of Charles IV the Golden Age came to an unfortunate and premature end. Not only was his eldest son who succeeded him, Václav IV, incompetent and ineffective, but religious dissension divided the country, a problem which was to beset the Czech Lands for centuries to come. As elsewhere in Europe an urge for church reform was in the air. Influenced by the teachings of Wycliff, Jan Hus raised the banner of reformation in Bohemia, and many Czechs rallied around him. In 1415 Hus was burnt at the stake in Constance as a heretic. But his doctrines did not die with him and unleashed the Hussite Wars (1419-36) in Bohemia, the first of Bohemia's many religious wars. Although some sort of compromise was achieved in the Compact of Basle, it is fair to say that Czech politics continued to be dominated – and confused – by religious issues for well over two centuries. For a short while it seemed as though Jiří z Poděbrad (who assumed power in 1452 and was King of Bohemia 1458-71) would stabilize matters to some extent, but after his death the Czechs turned to Poland for their kings – the 'Jagellon Kings' – which did not prove a happy choice, as their main interests lay elsewhere. So they let the Czechs get on with their private religious squabbles, which inevitably resulted in riots, lynchings and the like. With the end of the Jagellon dynasty the

Habsburgs took over in the person of Ferdinand I (1526-64), and from then onwards the Czech fortunes remained inextricably intertwined with the Habsburgs for virtually four centuries. Under Ferdinand I and his successor Maximilian II things were relatively peaceful, and when the crown passed to Maximilian's son Rudolf II (1577-1611), it even seemed at first as though a second Golden Age might be in store for Bohemia and Prague. However, under his reign the religious hatred flared up again. For let it not be forgotten: the Habsburgs were Catholics and, even when practising tolerance, would show preference to the Catholic nobility, whereas the Hussite and Utraquist religions were strongly dominated by nationalistic feelings and elements. But it was only after Rudolf's death, under his sucessor Matyáš, that matters came to a head.

In 1618 a number of Czech Protestant nobles had assembled in Prague; the situation became more and more tense, culminating in the famous *Prager Fenstersturz*, the Prague defenestration, when the Protestants stormed Prague Castle and threw three Catholic nobles, all three royal officials, out of the window. As they landed on a dung heap, the only hurt they suffered was that to their dignity; they could return to Vienna and complain – and so started the Thirty Years' War. In 1619, Matyáš died, and the Czechs elected the Protestant Palatine Count Friedrich von der Pfalz as King of Bohemia. He proved completely incapable, and as his reign only lasted for one year and four days, history has given him the nickname of 'Winter King'. When the Protestant and Catholic forces joined battle in earnest for the first time on 8 November 1620 at the White Mountain (*Bílá Hora*) the King awaited the outcome in Prague and, with his family, precipitately took to his heels as soon as he knew that the battle was lost. The Battle of the White Mountain put an end to the last vestige of Czech national freedom, a fact which was cruelly emphasized when Emperor Ferdinand II of Austria settled all accounts in 1621 and executed 27 of the rebellious Czech patriots in front of the old Prague Town Hall. For the next three hundred years, the Czechs were to remain a subjugated, Habsburg-dominated part of the Austrian Empire, and it is incredible how they maintained their individuality and preserved their national spirit.

Musically much of this period was barren. *Inter arma silent musae*, and neither Hussite wars nor Hussite doctrines were conducive to producing much music, certainly not along the lines of gay dances and drinking songs. But one tune emerged from those days which has remained with the Czech people as did the *Hospodine* and the *Svatý Václave*: the *Ktož jsú boží bojovníci*, 'Ye who are the warriors of God', that mighty Hussite hymn which, supposedly, was written by an ordinary soldier in the army of the great Hussite general Žižka. It therefore must stem from the early part of the 15th century, and no greater Czech melody was written for the next four hundred years, until František Škroup wrote the incidental music for *Fidlovačka* which incorporated the *Kde domov můj?*, 'Where is my Home?', which became the Czech National Anthem in 1918 and still is to the present day.

The advent of Ferdinand I in 1526 brought a new cultural life. Inspired by the example of their King, the noblemen of Bohemia began to establish their own private Chapels and bands, and although many of the musicians were imports from foreign parts, they laid a foundation for the future of Czech music by filling their libraries with compositions of Palestrina, Orlando di Lasso, Phillipe de Monte and others – in fact, with all the highest musical creations of their time. This led to a re-awakening of the inherent love for music of the Bohemian people and eventually to the foundation of educational music institutions. The basis which Charles IV had laid was bearing new fruit, and to this day Czech music is profiting by it.

Once the Battle of the White Mountain was lost, the doom of Bohemia was sealed. During the remaining 28 years of that Thirty Years' War it became the plaything of everyone's whim. Its nobility had been either massacred, expropriated or exiled, and although a few noble families continued to produce leaders, they were deluged by non-Bohemian families who were assiduously settled there by the Habsburgs. The country itself became a battle arena for anyone who wanted a battle; by 1648 more than a hundred cities and over 1000 villages lay in ruins, and the Czech Lands had lost a quarter of their population. It was a war in which Catholics and Protestants fought each other – what price Christianity?

During the second half of the 17th century there was little cause for rejoicing anywhere in the Czech Lands. The Austrian emperors had only one interest in Bohemia: how much they could exact by way of taxes. The nobility in Bohemia followed suit and extorted every penny and the last ounce of energy from their serfs. This naturally led to a number of minor peasants' revolts which all terminated in the same way: the ringleaders were taken and duly hanged, and if the ringleaders could not be found, some other peasants were hanged in their stead. It was also a dark period for learning and the arts. Although the German Governor of Bohemia, Prince Liechtenstein (himself a Protestant who had converted to Catholicism), did not actually succeed in destroying Prague University, he nevertheless expelled all Protestant professors who refused to turn Catholic, fused the University with the Jesuit College, and from then on the University was virtually a theological institution. It is not surprising that emigration became the order of the day, and so we come to this strange phenomenon: that for well over a hundred years music in Bohemia itself was in the doldrums, whilst Bohemian musicians could be found everywhere in Europe and played a large part in shaping the course of western music.

Before dealing with this latter aspect, however, we must review the internal Bohemian situation as far as music and musicians are concerned. Up to the advent of Emperor Charles VI (1711-40) the noble households still had their private orchestras, but under Charles VI 'the Habsburg neglect of the Czech kingdom reached its peak' (J.F.N. Bradley). The many Czech nobles who had moved to Vienna and occupied important positions at Court and in the Cabinet had little thought for their compatriots at home and did nothing to alleviate the situation in their native lands. On the other hand some of the wealthiest Czech nobles who had stayed behind – the Lobkovici, the Černíns, the Valdštejns – were virtually ruined and bankrupt, and there was no more money to engage musicians.

Yet music is an essential part of the Czech way of life, and music-making and musical education did go on throughout the whole of the 18th century. Music formed an important part of school education, and it is interesting to read Burney's report on that subject when he tells of his European travels in the 1770s. But the primary object of this musical training – forgetting for the moment about the pure inherent joy of learning and making music – was not to produce professional musicians, although some were still needed in the churches as singers and organists, but to prepare the young people for life. It was virtually impossible in those days to obtain a position in an aristocratic household without playing at least one instrument, for from the circle of his servants the nobleman gathered his band: the chief cook played the clarinet, the head gardener the trumpet, and the principal forester the horn (what else?). For those who did not want to go into service only two possibilities remained: either to go into the teaching profession, which was badly paid, or to become an itinerant musician. And let nothing be said against those bands of itinerant Bohemian musicians: they preserved and upheld the traditions of folk-song and folk-dance, they earned high praise from men as disparate as Spontini and Wagner, and they were welcomed with open arms outside the closer confines of their country when they turned up for special occasions – such as at the biannual Leipzig Fair, where they were constant visitors and their arrival gave the signal that Fair Time had started. But any musician who wanted to make a real name for himself had to go abroad.

To revert to historical matters for one moment: Charles VI died in 1740 and was succeeded by his daughter Maria Theresia. Friedrich II (Frederick the Great) of Prussia promptly started the First Silesian War (1740-42), in the course of which Kurfürst Karl Albert of Bavaria joined the Prussians and their French allies, invaded Bohemia and was crowned in Prague as Charles VII – one of the very few occasions in history that Prussia and Bavaria were allies in a war. In the Second Silesian War (1744–45) Frederick the Great himself invaded Bohemia and took Prague, and Charles VII died. The Seven Years' War (1756-63) again saw the Prussians in Bohemia, so altogether the Bohemians did not have too peaceful a time during the middle of the 18th century, even though the feud was essentially a Prusso-Austrian affair, but the Bohemians suffered consequent privations. And so things went on until the end of the century, until the gale that was unleashed at the Bastille on 14 July 1789 also began to waft a wind of change into the Czech Lands, giving Bohemians the first inkling of a new dawn to come.

It is impossible, within this context, to go into details regarding the many Czech musicians who left their home country during this period, nor is it possible to give anything like a complete and comprehensive picture. Let a few names and examples suffice. One of the earliest of the *émigrés* was Heinrich Ignaz Franz von Biber (1644-1704), a violinist and composer who went to Salzburg and, as conductor at the Archiepiscopal Court, was a predecessor in office of Wolfgang Amadeus Mozart. Jan (Johann) Dismas Zelenka (1679-1745) was another Bohemian musician who went to Vienna to study with Johann Joseph Fux and eventually became *Hofkapellmeister* in Dresden, and in a way he laid the foundations for that Dresden tradition which is still flourishing to the present day. Somewhat later, and of greater importance, is Bohuslav Matěj Černohorský (1684-1742), who was such an outstanding teacher that he gained the nickname of *Il padre Boemo*. Many of the later Czech composers were his pupils, and reputedly he taught Gluck and Tartini. He travelled widely and died in Graz. Among the most famous Bohemian musician-families are those of Benda and Stamic. Four sons of Jan Jiří Benda (1685-1757), a weaver and talented amateur musician, went to

Potsdam to the Court of Frederick the Great and were instrumental in furthering the musical life of the Prussian capital. The most important of them is Jiří Antonín (Georg)* (1722-95) who started his career in Potsdam, but then moved on to the Court of Gotha, where he remained for 28 years. During this time he travelled to Italy, and after he left the Court at Gotha his journeys took him to Hamburg, Vienna, Paris and Mannheim. As the name of Benda is ever associated with Potsdam and Berlin, so is the name of Stamic with Mannheim. The father, Jan Václav (Johann Wenzel Stamitz) (1717-57) went there at the age of 24 and can be considered the founder of the Mannheim School of orchestral playing and composition, a school which was to have such profound influence on both Haydn and Mozart. His son Karel was born in Mannheim and is generally considered to be part of the Mannheim School, but he left at the age of eleven to go to Strasbourg and then travelled widely all over Europe. However, in sheer genius he never came anywhere near his father.

Of Černohorský's Czech pupils the outstanding two are Jan (Johann) Zach (1699-1773) and František (Franz) Tůma. Zach, violinist and organist, went to Mainz and became the successor of Jan Ondráček, and his instrumental music is already permeated by the spirit of Czech folk-music. Tůma continued his studies in Vienna under Fux, eventually became Kapellmeister to the Dowager Empress Elisabeth, and as a boy chorister Haydn became acquainted with his compositions. Then there is František Václav (Franz Wenzel) Habermann (1706-83) who travelled widely in Italy, Spain and France and was not without influence on Handel; nor must we forget Franz Xaver Richter (1709-89), who belonged to the Mannheim School and eventually also moved to Strasbourg. One of the most amusing cases is that of Josef Mysliveček

*As Czech names and their pronunciation proved something of a problem to non-Czech-speaking people, most of the Bohemian composers adapted their names to local circumstances in one way or another – hence the many variants in parentheses.

(1737-81): he was a pupil of Habermann's, but then he spent practically his whole life in Italy, where he became the rage. His name proved completely unpronounceable to the Italians, so he was known as Venatorini or, more familarly, *Il divino Boemo*. The Mozarts, father and son, made his acquaintance in Bologna on one of their Italian journeys, and Wolfgang Amadeus still visited him in Munich in 1777, when he was in hospital suffering from a venereal disease which put an end to his life four years later.

To what extent Bohemian musicians roamed over the whole of Europe is perhaps best exemplified by Jan Ladislav Dusík (1760-1812) – not to be confused with František Xaver Dušek (Duschek) (1731-99) who lived in Prague most of his life apart from a brief study sojourn in Vienna and became a friend of Mozart's in Prague at the time of *Don Giovanni*. Dusík's travels (incidentally, in France and England he was known as Dussek or Dusseck) read like a tourist brochure: Austria, Amsterdam, Den Haag, Hamburg (where he had lessons from C.P.E. Bach), Berlin, St. Petersburg, Paris, Italy, back to Paris (where he had to leave when the French Revolution broke out), twelve years in London, Hamburg, Magdeburg, and eventually back to France. Despite the fact that most of his work was done abroad, he had a stronger influence on Czech music than is generally supposed, and traces of it can even be found in Dvořák's *Stabat Mater*.

Then there was Antonín Rejcha (Anton, Antoine Reicha) (1770-1836) who, in the course of his travels, was in touch with Haydn, Mozart and Beethoven as well as Salieri and Albrechtsberger. Finally he settled in Paris and eventually became Boieldieu's successor at the *Institut*. Of the many composers who settled in Vienna (possibly in the wake of the Czech nobles who became 'imperialized' at the Vienna Court) three men must not be forgotten: Florian Leopold Gassmann (1729-74), Antonín Vranický (Anton Wranitzky) (1761-1820) and Jan Hugo Voříšek (Worzischek) (1791-1825). Gassmann studied in Italy, became Gluck's successor in Vienna as a ballet composer and conductor, and was the founder of the

Tonkünstler-Societät. His pupil was Salieri – the man who, in the Vienna of his time, was considered superior to Mozart. Vranický, who studied with Haydn, Mozart and Albrechtsberger, eventually became *Kapellmeister* to Prince Lobkowitz in Vienna and, considering how important Weber was to become in the operatic life of Prague, it is one of those quirks of fate that Vranický's daughter Karoline was to be the Agathe in the first performance of *Der Freischütz*. Voříšek knew Beethoven well; he was on friendly terms with Hummel, Meyerbeer and Moscheles; as a composer he represents a transition between Beethoven and Schubert – and there can be little doubt that Schubert was influenced by Voříšek's *Impromptus*.

This is by no means the whole list of Czech musicians who lived and worked outside Bohemia, but on the other hand let us not overlook two who stayed in Prague: František Xaver Brixi (1732-71) and Václav Jan Tomášek (1774-1850). Brixi became choirmaster at the Cathedral of St. Vitus at the age of 27. He was a prolific composer with a distinctive style which clearly foreshadows Mozart. Tomášek – organist, composer and teacher – knew Beethoven and was strongly influenced by him. He had a flair for the dramatic (hence his nickname 'the Schiller of Music') and, in turn, exerted *his* influence on Schubert and Schumann.

The year 1789 has already been mentioned. There was hardly a country in Europe where the political, social and humanitarian impact of the French Revolution did not make itself felt, and Bohemia was no exception. Nationalism in those days went hand in hand with the emancipation of the individual, and the Czechs proudly began to raise their heads again despite the Habsburgs. They had their successes. At Prague University a Chair of Czech Language was established, and 1809 saw the publication of the first comprehensive Czech grammar. Father Pubička not only had his 'History of the Czech Kingdom' published, but had it published at government expense. Nevertheless these were only the first tender shoots, and the realization of the ultimate dream of all Czech patriots had to wait until 1918.

But just as the French Revolution was that great political turning point, there was also a cultural, musical turning point: in 1786 Mozart's *Le Nozze di Figaro* had its first performance outside Austria in Prague, and in 1787, again in Prague, the première of *Don Giovanni* took place and was received with tremendous ovations. As usual, Vienna had failed to recognize the native genius living within its walls (as was to be the case with Bruckner less than a century later), and it was Prague which truly realized what Mozart meant – indeed, it is difficult to decide whether we should speak of 'Mozart's Prague' or 'Prague's Mozart'. There can be little doubt that, of the audiences which heard Mozart's operas, the vast majority belonged to the Austro-German aristocracy, but it is also reported that throughout the streets of Prague everybody was humming, whistling, singing the great tunes from *Figaro* and *Don Giovanni*. Admittedly, the Mozart cult which started at that time also had the unfortunate consequence that there were Czech musicians who became dyed-in-the-wool reactionaries and refused so much as to consider 'avant-garde' composers such as Beethoven, but this was only a secondary and negligible result.

Only a few decades later the nationalistic spirit of the French Revolution received a further impulse during the Napoleonic Wars, and musically another great impact was provided by Carl Maria von Weber, who spent the years 1813-16 in Prague as director and conductor of the Opera. Weber's approach to music was always open and forward-looking, and under his directorship Prague came to hear operas not only by Mozart, but also works by Méhul, Cherubini, Grétry, Meyerbeer, Spontini and many others. It was Weber who gave the first performance of Spohr's opera *Faust* in Prague and performed Beethoven's *Fidelio* (in its final version of 1814) on 21 November 1814, a matter of six months after the opera's first performance in Vienna. How seriously Weber took his work in

Prague can be gauged by the fact that he took the trouble to learn the Czech language in order to reach a better understanding with his musicians.

These influences combined in shaping the political as well as the cultural life in Bohemia. Czech nationalism was strengthened and, though the revolution of 1848 proved abortive as far as Bohemia was concerned and the people had to wait until 1918 for their national freedom, there were strong trends in the cultural life pointing towards a brighter future. From 1806 onwards newspapers in Czech began to appear, at first only sporadically, but later with greater regularity, and Czech writers such as K.J. Erben and Gustav Pfleger-Moravský came to the fore. Czech painters still largely worked abroad, but a new national school of painting was called into being in Bohemia itself by Josef Mánes, and Josef Kajetán Tyl became the founder of Czech theatre.

On the musical side the two names of special import are Jan Jakub Ryba (1765-1815) and Karel (Pavel) Křížkovský (1820-85). Ryba was the first to compose songs to Czech texts by Czech poets (ironically enough, they were published under a German title as *Böhmische Lieder*) and Křížkovský was the first composer to combine a classical style of composition with knowledge and insight into Bohemian folk-music. As such he can be considered the true forerunner of Smetana. But before we come to Smetana himself, a word must also be said about František Jan Škroup (1801-62). In 1826 he composed *Dráteník* ('The Tinker') which can rightly be considered the first true Czech opera. However, his chief claim to fame will always rest on the music which he wrote in 1834 for Tyl's farcical play *Fidlovačka* which, as has already been mentioned, contains the song *Kde domov můj*. He also held the post of chief conductor at the Prague *Ständetheater* (1827-57), where he introduced Wagner and other 'controversial modern composers' to the Prague audiences. Eventually he lost his post, had to emigrate, and died in poverty in Rotterdam.

All these events, all these men paved the way and set the scene for that giant amongst Czech nationalist musicians who was born in Litomyšl in Bohemia on 2 March 1824: Bedřich Smetana. He was the son of a brewer, a profession which, as everyone knows, was highly esteemed in Bohemia and has largely contributed to its renown. Much against the will of his father he became a musican, and when still in his teens, he combined his gifts as a pianist with his feeling for Bohemian folk-dances to make himself a popular figure in the social world of Pilsen (Plzeň) where he was then going to school. But his studies as a composer only began seriously in Prague in 1843, where he studied with Josef Proksch until 1846. Almost all his early works are compostions for the piano; it was the revolution of 1848 which brought about his first orchestral works. To what extent Smetana was directly involved in that revolution is not known for certain: what we do know is that he was filled with the most ardent nationalism and thought it wise to disappear from Prague to stay with his parents at Obříství until the excitement had died down. During this time he wrote patriotic marches as well as his first major orchestral work, the 'Festive Overture'. In the years to come he earned his living as a concert pianist and music teacher, but the oppressive atmosphere of the Prague of those days led him to embark on six years (1856-62) which can best be called his 'years of travel' during which he 'commuted' between Prague and Gothenburg in Sweden.

Smetana grew up with the music of Haydn, Mozart, Beethoven and Weber; his early piano music cannot deny the influence of Mendelssohn, Schumann and Chopin, and then he fell under the spell of Liszt, Berlioz, Wagner and the rest of the Neo-German school. *This* is the basis on which all his later work rests, and it is a tribute to his strength of character that he could fuse those diverse trends with his innate musical nationalism: that the result was truly Czech music of the highest order.

The main turning point in Smetana's life was 1862 when he again settled in Prague for good. Due to Italy's victories over the Austrians in 1859 the Habsburg rule over Bohemia was becoming somewhat relaxed, and his experiences in Sweden had brought the realization to Smetana that the goal of his ambitions lay in the sung word. In quick succession (1863-67) he produced his first three operas: 'The Brandenburgers in Bohemia' (*Braniboři v Čechách*), 'The Bartered Bride' (*Prodaná nevěsta*) and *Dalibor* – like the remaining five of his completed operas all based on subjects of Czech history, Czech folklore or Czech country life. Although to a certain extent he adopted Wagnerian principles (in the case of *Dalibor* one cannot help being reminded of *Lohengrin* in Act I) he steered clear of mythological and exaggerated symbolism, with the possible exception of *Libuše* which, in any case, was intended to be a ceremonial opera.

But side by side with his work as a composer Smetana was also active in practical fields: he became the conductor of the Hlahol Choral Society, was instrumental in the founding of the Society of Artists (*Umělecká beseda*), and from 1866 onwards he was conductor at the Czech Opera House in Prague, the Provisional Theatre (*Prozatímní Divadlo*) which had been opened in 1862. During the eight years of his activities there, until his hearing failed and he had to resign in 1874, Smetana struck a judicious balance between the old and the new, between Italian, German, French as well as Czech opera. It was during this period that a young viola player in the orchestra fell under Smetana's influence: Antonín Dvořák.

The last ten years of Smetana's life were overshadowed by that illness which first robbed him of his hearing and eventually of his reason, but nevertheless his creative energy remained relatively unimpaired until near his end, which came in May 1884 when he was sixty. These last ten years saw the birth of four more great operas as well as his finest orchestral work: the symphonic cycle *Má Vlast* ('My Country') (1874-79). Although the six tone poems were based on Lisztian concepts, they are nevertheless the purest musical expression of Bohemian nationalism at its truest and most sincere. Before our eyes – or should I say our ears? – passes the whole of

Bohemian folklore and landscape: the glories of the legendary castle *Vyšehrad* dominating Prague, the course of the river *Vltava* (Moldau), the heroic saga of *Šárka*, the beauty and gaiety of 'Bohemia's Meadows and Forests' (*Z čekých luhů a hájů*). Then comes *Tábor*, fortress of the Hussites, gloomy and tempestuous, with the Hussite chorale 'Ye who are the warriors of God' dominating the entire work from beginning to end. In *Blaník*, the sixth and last tone poem of the cycle, the melody wells up again. Blaník is that hill in which, according to Czech legend, the heroes of Hussite times are sleeping, as is Barbarossa according to the German *Kyffhäuser* myth, waiting for the day when their people will need them in the fight against oppression and for freedom. Smetana's music, after a pastoral interlude, breaks out into a rousing marching tune which – inevitably – is transmuted into a Polka, and when it is fused as a final culmination with the themes of the Hussite chorale, of *Vyšehrad* and of *Vltava*, the whole of Bohemia's glory bursts forth in a way which Smetana, and only Smetana, could achieve. After nine hundred years of music making, after nine hundred years of political ups and downs, it was Smetana who laid the rock-like foundation of a truly national style of Czech music. It is the solid basis on which Dvořák and after him men like Suk, Janáček and Martinů could safely build.

DVOŘÁK'S CHILDHOOD

Less than 15 miles north of Prague, on the banks of the River Vltava (Moldau), lies Nelahozeves (formerly Mühlhausen). It is a typical Bohemian village, dominated by a castle, reflecting the historical and cultural heritage of that area. Here Jan Nepomuk (1764-1842), the grandfather of 'our' Dvořák, set up as a butcher and was eventually succeeded by the tenth of his twelve children, František, who added an inn to the butcher's business, thereby creating that form of establishment which is so well-known and widespread in that particular area of central Europe: a *Gasthaus-Metzgerei*.

The Dvořáks (theirs is a name by no means uncommon in those parts) sprang from healthy Bohemian stock, and the butcher's trade seems to have run in the family. But side by side with this professional calling we find an equally strong trait: a love of music. Almost everyone of Dvořák's ancestors on the paternal side of his family was a proficient amateur performer on one or several instruments, his father František being acclaimed particularly as a zither player to the end of his days, although he was also a reasonable fiddler.

On his mother's side matters were somewhat different. Anna Zdeňková (1820-1882), as far as we can gather, had no particular musical leanings. She was born at Uhy, where her father was steward to Prince Lobkovic (Lobkowitz), and in her family the talents lay in embroidery and related handicrafts. František Dvořák and Anna Zdeňková were married on 17 November 1840, and they seem to have been ideally suited for each other. In the same way František must have been admirably suited to his profession, as his natural Bohemian bent for music-making must have endeared him to all his patrons, for in addition to his zither and violin playing he also had a beautiful baritone voice.

Like other members of their family they had many children, fourteen in all, of whom only eight survived early childhood. The first of these was Antonín, born in the *Gasthaus-Metzgerei* on 8 September 1841 and christened on the following day in the little church just across the road in a magnificent 16th-century font. Like his parents, he was baptized in the Roman Catholic faith, a faith to which he was to remain true and devout all his life without ever becoming bigotted.

Though he was not old enough to remember it later, the first major event in Toník's life – he was known as Toník to everybody in Nelahozeves – occurred when he was just ten months old. The inn caught fire and was gutted, and the family had to make a temporary home for themselves in the butcher's shop. However, the damage must have been repaired relatively quickly, for Antonín's first brother, František Serafín, was born at the inn on 3 February 1843.

Needless to say, the Dvořák parents doted on their first-born son and obviously expected him to follow in the family trade and tradition. But just as naturally the father's innate musicality asserted itself, and at an early age he taught Antonín the violin so that, as we are told, he could already entertain the inn's clientele at the age of five by playing dance-tunes on his fiddle. From earliest childhood he was steeped in Bohemian folk-music; the rhythms of *Furiant* and Polka, of *Sousedská* and *Skočná* got into his blood.

Even at that early age Dvořák must have been taken to the nearby Palais Veltrusy. This would have made a tremendous and lasting impression on him, especially the fountain displays, for these impressions later found their sublimation in his music, particularly in the operas *Jakobín*, 'The Devil and Kate' (Act III), *Rusalka* (Act II), as well as in his symphonic poem 'The Water Goblin' (*Vodník*).

When he was six years old, in autumn 1847, life began in earnest for young Antonín. He had to start school in Nelahozeves and came under the guidance of the kindly and easy-going village schoolmaster-*cum*-organist Josef Spitz. How good a teacher Spitz was we shall never know, for if he ever bothered to keep any records regarding his pupils' proficiency, these would have all been destroyed when the schoolhouse burnt down some years later. But two facts remain, one positive and one negative: Spitz realized the musical talent which Antonín had inherited from his father and furthered his singing and violin playing, so that even as a boy he could play in the village band and in church. Probably Spitz also gave him his first lessons in keyboard playing. On the other hand he neglected Antonín's German, a very serious matter in the Bohemia of those years immediately after the abortive nationalist uprising of 1848. At the village school Dvořák spent six years, until the summer of 1853. Although his musical talents were recognized and appreciated, Antonín was expected to follow in the family footsteps and now, aged almost twelve, he was apprenticed to his father to learn the butcher's trade. Nevertheless, as during his schooldays, he continued to play the violin and remained a favourite entertainer at his father's inn.

But there remained that shortcoming: lack of knowledge of the German language. Throughout his life Dvořák had an aversion to German which he always considered an alien tongue. In later life his correspondence and arguments with his publisher Simrock give ample evidence of this attitude. In those days of the Austro-Hungarian Empire, a knowledge of German was an essential requisite for any prospective innkeeper and so, to remedy this deficiency, Antonín was sent in 1854* to his maternal uncle Antonín Zdeněk at Zlonice. Uncle Zdeněk was steward to Count Kinsky and looked on young Antonín as if he were his own son, creating a 'home from home' for him. Dvořák joined the Zlonice Butchers' Guild as an apprentice to continue his professional training, and his general education was entrusted to the headmaster Josef Toman and the German teacher Antonín Liehmann (1808-79), both of them bilingual in Czech and German. Unfortunately (or, for posterity, fortunately) Toman was also a singer, choirmaster of the church, and played the organ, the violin and other instruments, while Liehmann was an outstanding amateur musician and theory teacher who was the church organist and also played the violin, the clarinet and the horn. So, inevitably, musical training soon became the most important aspect of the tuition which the young Dvořák received from his two mentors, and study of German receded into the background. Liehmann's teaching in particular had a profound influence on Antonín's musical development, and throughout his life he remembered him with respect and affection – later immortalizing him in his opera *Jakobín* as 'Benda', the kindly schoolmaster-*cum*-organist.

In 1855 the whole Dvořák family moved to Zlonice – about ten miles, as the crow flies, to the north-west of Nelahozeves – at the advice of Uncle Zdeněk, who was of the opinion that an inn in the 'large' town would be a more profitable business than the *Gasthaus-Metzgerei* in a village. So František Dvořák became the leaseholder of the *Velká Hospoda,* 'The Big Inn'. The enterprise was not crowned with success, however: his predecessor promptly opened up a similar establishment opposite, took most of his customers with him, and by 1860 František Dvořák was bankrupt and had to give up his lease. It was only natural that, with his father taking over the 'Big Inn', Antonín should move back in with the family, but the next year seems to have been far from happy for him: it was soon realized that music had pushed German and his training as a

---

*Whenever authorities differ on a date, I have adhered to information provided by Jarmil Burghauser in his *Thematic Catalogue* (Appendix 'Survey of the Life of Antonín Dvořák') or given to me personally by Dr. Karel Mikysa.

butcher into the background, and his father tightened the reins, much to the displeasure and grief of Antonín. Nevertheless, on 1 November 1856, he obtained his Journeyman's Certificate from the Butcher's Guild.* By this time, now 15 years old, he had already decided in his own mind that he wanted to be a professional musician. Liehmann supported him in this, but his father – much though he loved music – was adamant that his eldest son should be trained in a profession which would guarantee him a secure livelihood, and accordingly sent him off to Česká Kamenice (then Böhmisch-Kamnitz), a town at the foot of the Lausitz mountains in the Sudetenland, to learn German properly. There he attended the town school and studied music on the side with the church organist František Hanke. However, as the area was almost entirely German-speaking, he had little option but to learn the language, and in July 1857 he returned to Zlonice with both the Leaving Certificate of the Česká Kamenice school and a reasonable knowledge of German. On his return Liehmann again urged František Dvořák to let the boy become a musician; it was presumably then that Dvořák made his first public appearance on the organ of the main church of Zlonice. But now Uncle Zdeněk supported Liehmann, at the same time offering some material assistance to finance Antonín's musical studies. So, in September 1857, young Dvořák set off for Prague.

*This is the date given by Burghauser. Clapham gives the date as 2 November and also casts some doubts on the authenticity of that Certificate. In view of Dvořák's later achievements, these questions would not appear to be of overwhelming importance.

FORMATIVE YEARS

Prague was the Mecca of his dreams, and for the rest of his life
Prague was to remain his musical home. On arrival he found
lodgings with a cousin in the Old Town of Prague,
Dominikánska Ulice No. 238, but conditions were not
particularly congenial. Roughly one year later he moved in with
his aunt Josefa Dušková (his father's sister) and her husband
Václav Dušek, a railway employee, in Karlovo Náměsti No.
558, where he was much happier. On the whole it can be said
that his relatives came to his aid during those early and difficult
years in a most generous manner, and young Dvořák was
grateful despite certain drawbacks to which we shall refer
later. Aunt Josefa (or Josefina) offered him what we would
now call 'bed and breakfast' with one additional meal thrown in
on special family occasions.

In the Prague of those days there were two main musical
institutions: the Conservatorium and the Organ School. The
former was then intent on turning out virtuosos rather than
musicians, and so, at the advice of his mentor Liehmann, he
enrolled as a pupil at the Organ School. At that time it was
under the German directorship of Karl Pitsch, but his teachers
were Czechs. This had a great bearing on his future attitude to
music: Josef Foerster taught him the organ, Josef Zvonař
singing, and František Blažek theory. It goes without saying

that those student years in Prague were very hard for Antonín, despite the assistance he received from his parents, from Uncle Zdeněk and through the generosity of his relatives in Prague as regards lodgings. His studies were also hampered by his reticence to speak German, for this was the official language at the Organ School. He soon overcame this deficiency, though, by taking an additional language course, and, on the financial side, eked out his scant allowance by working as an 'extra' in various bands and orchestras as a viola player.

The big drawback of living at Aunt Josefa's was the absence of a piano. However, at the Organ School he had made friends with Karel Bendl, a student in his third year with whom Dvořák was to entertain the closest ties of friendship until Bendl's death in 1897. Bendl was much better off than Antonín and generously allowed him free access to his library of classical scores, as well as letting him use his piano whenever Dvořák felt so inclined. But it is difficult to keep imposing on a friend, and this led Dvořák to make another change of abode a few years later.

In the autumn of 1858 he began the second year of his studies at the Organ School, an advanced course, and obtained his Leaving Certificate in July 1859. Quite apart from the sound musical knowledge he acquired from his teachers during those two years, his musical horizons were also widened considerably by the concerts and operas which he was able to hear. But he rarely had sufficient money to pay admission charges and, as often as not, he had to scrounge around for a ticket or try to smuggle his way in somehow or other. But apart from attending performances, he also gained much insight into the music of his day through his activity as a viola player in the orchestra of the St. Cecilia Society, which he probably joined in November 1857. This orchestra was under the direction of Antonín Apt, a fervent admirer of Wagner and Liszt, composers at whom the Organ School looked askance. The young Dvořák was fired by Apt's enthusiasm, and this marks the beginning of that period when he came under the spell of the Neo-German school – an influence which it took him many years, if not to shake off, then at least to absorb into his own highly personal style.

Dvořák was almost 18 years old when he completed his training at the Organ School, but as he received his Leaving Certificate the financial assistance from Uncle Zdeněk also came to an end. Now he had to stand on his own two feet and make up his mind about the future course of his life. First he did the conventional thing: he applied for the position of organist at St. Henry's Church (*Sv. Jindřich*), but his application was rejected. He then decided to take the risk of supporting himself as a free-lance musician, an unusual procedure in those days. Apart from playing in the orchestra of the St. Cecilia Society, he also joined the orchestra of Karel Komzák, again as a viola player. (In his Zlonice days the viola had become his favourite instrument next to the organ.) With the Komzák band he played almost nightly in various Prague restaurants – a repertoire of overtures and popular medleys from the operas – and so he could at the same time enlarge his knowledge of music and earn a meagre living.

For almost fourteen years from the time he left the Organ School, Dvořák's life was fraught with decision-making and financial worries, as well as heart-break, but as far as one can gather his days followed a pattern of an unexciting yet strenuous routine. Each morning was filled with rehearsals of the Komzák band, each evening with performances, and during his free afternoons he studied scores, probably also did a certain amount of composition, as well as teaching to add to his income. Events of note are few and far between.

Of these few events, the one which was to have a deep influence on Dvořák's life was the formation of the Czech National Theatre, which came into being on 18 November 1862. Up till then Prague only had the German Provincial Theatre which concentrated in the main on German, Italian and French Opera. With the advent of the National Theatre, whose bold, declared aim it was to produce Czech operas (or at least to produce all operas in the Czech language) the

German Provincial Theatre now had a rival – and this proved to be exceedingly fruitful. As the National Theatre* took over the Komzák Orchestra completely, Dvořák naturally became a member of the National Theatre Orchestra from the very beginning. At times the orchestras of the two theatres also forgot their rivalry and joined forces to give concerts, and Dvořák gained much new and valuable experience. The list of concert programmes and operas in which Dvořák played the viola is astounding. Already in 1858 he had played in concerts conducted by Franz Liszt, on 8 February 1863 he played under Richard Wagner himself in a concert of Wagner's works, and in the National Theatre he participated in first performances of many Czech operas (such as Smetana's 'Brandenburgers in Bohemia', 'The Bartered Bride', *Dalibor*) as well as of operas in the Czech language. When Smetana was appointed director of the National Theatre, in September 1866, Dvořák was brought into closer contact with the man who had such a decisive influence on Czech music and who directed his ideas into new channels.

On the personal front the only major change in the routine of his life was that, early in 1864, he moved in with Mořic Anger, a friend of his and a fellow-member of the orchestra, who was already sharing a flat with four others. One of these was Karel Čech, the brother of Adolf Čech who had shared a desk with Dvořák in the orchestra of the St. Cecilia Society and who later, as a conductor, was to become such a fervent advocate of Dvořák's music. These young men together in one

*It was, of course, the hope of the newly formed Czech National Theatre to have a home of its own, but this dream was not to be realized for many years. The foundation stone for the *Narodní Divadlo* ('National Theatre') was not laid until 16 May 1868, on which occasion Smetana's *Dalibor* had its first performance. The National Theatre was inaugurated on 11 June 1881 with the première of Smetana's *Libuše*, but burnt down as early as 12 August of that year before having been put to regular use. It was then rebuilt, and the 're-inauguration' took place on 18 November 1883 with another performance of *Libuše*. Up until that time, performances had taken place in the *Prozatímní Divadlo* ('Provisional Theatre'). In this text the term 'National Theatre' will be used, however, as referring to the *organization* and not the physical structure of the building.

apartment – it must have been a real *vie de Bohème*, a style of life not truly suited to Dvořák's nature. But there was an inestimable advantage: there was a piano which Dvořák could use whenever he so wished. However, in the long run the whole arrangement proved not to Dvořák's liking, and in October 1865 he moved back in with Aunt Josefa. Probably this return to her flat in Karlovo Náměsti was also prompted by the fact that his earnings were by now sufficient to enable him to hire a piano.

Early in that same year 1865 another event took place which, though at the time it may have appeared a minor matter, was to have the most far-reaching effect on Dvořák's whole life and was indeed to shape his destiny. Jan Čermák, a wealthy goldsmith, engaged him as piano teacher for his daughter Josefina. Dvořák promptly fell violently in love with his pupil. His love was not returned – even though he tried to woo her with his music, in particular the song cycle 'Cypresses'. Dvořák, after suffering the agonies of unrequited love, eventually accepted his fate, but matters did not end there. He found his affections transferring to Josefina's younger sister Anna, and later, in 1873, he married her, while Josefina married Václav Count Kaunic (Wenzel Graf Kaunitz) in 1877. The couples remained on the closest and friendliest terms to the end of their days, and it was through Count Kaunic, in later years, that it became possible for Dvořák to fulfil one of his fondest dreams: to own a little house in the country.

Dvořák's teaching activities must have increased considerably during those years, for in July 1871 he could afford to resign from the orchestra of the National Theatre of which he had been Principal Viola for nine years. But these activities were not only important from the purely material angle. In January 1873 he was engaged as piano teacher to the Neff family, and it was at their instigation that he eventually composed the Moravian Duets – those pieces with which he was first to establish a reputation outside Czechoslovakia.

We must now look at the compositions which Dvořák produced during those early years, and from the very beginning let us face the fact that Dvořák was no infant prodigy. Dvořák's very first composition (and that is the only reason for mentioning it) stems from the Zlonice days: the 'Forget-me-not' Polka of 1855/56, and even this is only a little Polka written around a Trio by Liehmann. Apart from some organ pieces which he wrote as exercises during his student days, there are no extant compositions until we come to 1861, for anything which he may have written in those intervening years has either been lost, or destroyed by Dvořák himself. The first compositions that we still possess are a String Quintet in A minor (op.1) and a String Quartet in A major (op.2) of 1862. Dvořák himself must have attached some importance to these works, as they were the first which he thought worthy of being given opus numbers.

There is a gap of three years between the String Quartet mentioned above and his next composition: his Symphony No.1 in C minor, known as the 'Bells of Zlonice' * of 1865. It is a somewhat long-winded composition and of little merit. However, it has had a curious history – Dvořák sent the score to Germany as an entry for a competition: he won no prize and the score was never returned. It finally came to light in 1923. But Dvořák himself seems never to have set much store by the work for when, a good few years later, one of his students asked him how he had reacted when the symphony was lost, he simply said: 'Well, I just sat down and wrote another one'. As he thought the score had vanished for good, he allocated to all his future symphonies a number which is one less than that which actually corresponds to the truth. It is also of interest that persons old enough to remember the days before 1914 (the original church bells of Zlonice were melted down during World War I) say that one bell was cracked, resulting in a

*The title 'The Bells of Zlonice' (*Zlonické zvony*) does not appear on the title page of the MS, but we are told that verbally Dvořák referred to the Symphony by that name. In writing it only occurs in a list of compositions which he sketched out for V.J. Novotný in 1887 or 1888.

slightly discordant peal. One is tempted to assume that Dvořák had this in mind when writing certain dissonances in the first movement of his symphony.

When in 1865 he became the piano teacher of Josefina Čermákova and fell in love with her, this must have been a spur to his creative aspirations. He followed up the Symphony with a Cello Concerto in A which, however, never got beyond the 'cello with piano' stage.* Of more importance is the cycle of eighteen songs which he wrote to texts by Gustav Pfleger-Moravský under the title of 'Cypresses' *(Cypřiše)* and with which he tried to win his beloved Josefina. The songs in themselves are in no way overwhelming (and, according to Burghauser, have never yet been performed in their entirety in their original form) but they must have meant a great deal to Dvořák, for throughout his creative life he kept returning to them, arranging them for instrumental combinations, or using their melodies or fragments of them in other works.

Next in 1865 came another symphony (No. 2 in B flat). This also suffers from diffuseness, and the influences of Wagner and Liszt are perhaps too evident.Although its opening is truly symphonic in concept, he just could not maintain the verve of its beginning, and it soon loses its initial impact. Then came some songs and orchestral Interludes (such as were probably required for theatrical performances), and after three years of barrenness he embarked on what was up to then his most ambitious project: an opera *Alfred.* More will have to be said about this work when we look at Dvořák's operas, but it is typical of his taciturn nature that he settled down to the composition without telling anyone about it, and when it was completed he made no attempts to get *Alfred* staged. In later years he revised only the overture, calling it 'Tragic Overture'.

*The manuscript for this work was not discovered until after 1918, and in 1929 Günther Raphael made a performance version of it which, however, was not particularly Dvořákian. More recently a new reconstruction has come into being. The solo part has been slightly revised by the Czech cellist Miloš Sádlo, and Jarmil Burghauser has orchestrated Dvořák's piano accompaniment. This new realization deserves full commendation.

In this form it had its first performance in 1905 and was published by Simrock in 1912 with the title 'Dramatic Overture'. The opera as such had to wait for a stage performance until 1938.

At about the same period he also composed three String Quartets (in B flat, D, and E minor) which, however, have only been re-discovered relatively recently. They all owe a great debt to Wagner and only the instrumental parts have survived. Dvořák was undoubtedly referring to these quartets when, in 1887, he listed works which he had burnt or otherwise destroyed. It is, however, worth mentioning that, of the three quartets under discussion the last, in E minor, was written in one continuous movement and certainly betrays shades of *Tristan*. These quartets Dvořák followed up in 1871 by another opera, 'King and Charcoal Burner', which again will be discussed later. Then came some songs, two Piano Trios (which he later burnt), and in the first half of 1872 he composed his *Hymnus* 'The Heirs of the White Mountain'.

Apart fom this *Hymnus*, all these early compositions are mainly of academic interest. Even though quite a number of them are now available in print, they are but rarely performed, and for very good reasons. For one, the hand of Wagner lies heavily on them; for another, Dvořák had not yet reached any sort of true maturity as a composer. As far as his ideas of form were concerned, particularly in his instrumental works, his models were to be the Viennese classics, Beethoven and Schubert, and later Brahms. Melodic invention was to be Dvořák's most immediately remarkable gift, and he can take his place beside Schubert and Tchaikovsky. Kurt Honolka quotes Brahms as having said: 'That chap has more ideas than any of us. Everyone else could glean together main subjects from out of his left-overs.' Unfortunately in his early compositions Dvořák was unable to mould his melodic inspiration into a taut form. The structure is weakened, and to many of these early works the term 'garrulous' could be applied.

INTERLUDIUM I:
DVOŘÁK AND OPERA

The subject of Dvořák and opera must be looked at more closely, divorced from the tracing of his life-story. As with Schubert, it was Dvořák's most cherished ambition to become a composer of operas of international repute – an ambition which persued him to the end of his life and which was never really to be fulfilled. We have here one of those unhappy but not infrequent cases of a parent doting most on the weakest child. Audiences are often better judges of works than their composers. Of the former Carl Maria von Weber once said: 'Individually every one of them is an ass, but as a whole they are the Voice of God' – *vox populi, vox Dei*. Dvořák placed all his faith in his operas, but music lovers all over the world have decided otherwise. Like Schubert again, he was bedevilled by bad or inadequate libretti; besides, one cannot escape the feeling that Dvořák lacked the sense of stage such as was possessed by the truly great operatic composers. All his operas (except for the very early ones) contain a wealth of melodic invention, but the simple fact remains that this hybrid form of art called 'opera' does not depend on the quality of the music alone – it also depends on the story element, the libretto, and the visual, and somehow all these factors must add up to produce an organic whole: *Theatre.*

All in all Dvořák composed eleven operas – if we omit the

Overture and Incidental Music to *Josef Kajetán Tyl* and count
the two versions of 'King and Charcoal Burner' as two
separate operas, as the so-called 'second version' is a
completely new setting of a revised libretto. The first two of
these eleven operas have already been mentioned. For *Alfred*,
which he wrote between May and October 1870, he chose for
his libretto the drama *Alfred der Grosse* by Theodor Körner, a
patriotic German poet of the Napoleonic Wars; this was the
first and only time in his life that Dvořák made use of a libretto
in German. Körner's drama is mercifully forgotten, even in
Germany, and so is Dvořák's opera. But he did what others
have done before and since: he chose an episode from the
history of another country to stand for his own. In *Alfred* he
equated the brave English with the Bohemians and the
darstardly Danes with the Habsburgs. But Dvořák's capa-
bilities were nowhere near ready for such an undertaking, and
the music, despite certain Bohemian elements, is a frantic and
futile effort of holding the whole thing together by Wagnerian
Leitmotive.

For his next operatic venture, 'King and Charcoal Burner'
(*Král a uhlíř*) which he completed in December 1871, he chose
a text by Bernard J. Lobeský, the *nom de plume* of a notary,
Bernard Guldener. It is a comic opera, and here Dvořák
entered the realm to which he was to adhere for all his other
operas except the very last: the realm of Slavonic folklore and
history. This time Dvořák must have been surer of himself, for
he submitted the score to Smetana who, however, returned it
to him without comment. But the older composer cannot have
been completely unimpressed, for on 14 April 1872 he
conducted its overture in a Philharmonic Concert in Prague. It
was the first time that an orchestral work of Dvořák was
performed in public, and that his name appeared in print on a
programme. After Dvořák had scored his first real success
with the *Hymnus*, the National Theatre accepted 'King and
Charcoal Burner' for production, but after a number of
rehearsals it was rejected as unperformable, which mortified
and depressed him unutterably and caused him to scan his

earlier output with severe self-criticism. The result was a wholesale destruction of older compositions.

What Dvořák did during the months April-November 1874 is incredible and must be a unique event in the entire history of opera compostion. Having talked Guldener (alias Lobeský) into revising the libretto of 'King and Charcoal Burner', he settled down to the task of composing the whole opera from scratch. It must be stressed again that this was in no way a 'revision' of the first version of 1871: he made no use of any of the former musical material, and started his move away from Wagnerian concepts. He was now tending more towards the simpler style of composers like Weber, whose wealth of folklike melodies was much better suited to Dvořák's creative personality. However, the libretto remained poor, and even a further revision (which he undertook in 1887) could not really save the opera. But this time it did get four performances at the National Theatre – in November 1874. Incidentally, it always remains a matter of amazement to me, not only in the case of this particular opera, how little time elapsed between the completion of the score and the first performance. After all, the parts had to be copied out and the works rehearsed – how *did* they do it?

When 'King and Charcoal Burner' had its first performance, Dvořák was already at work on 'The Stubborn Lovers' (*Tvrdé palice*), a one-act comic opera with a libretto by Josef Štolba, a Bohemian rustic comedy. Dvořák completed the work on Christmas Eve 1874. Perhaps he was influenced in choosing his subject by the success of Smetana's 'Two Widows' earlier that year. Although 'The Stubborn Lovers' is charming in many ways and represents a further move away from Wagner, it had to wait until 1881 for its first performance. This was, perhaps, because it is notoriously difficult to place a one-act opera in the repertoire.

We now come to Dvořák's next – and perhaps most unfortunate – opera, *Vanda*, an effort in five acts (three would have been ample!) based on a Polish legend. Dvořák's choice of subject matter may have been caused by the pro-Polish feeling in Czechoslovakia at the time. However, when the first performance took place in April 1876, this general feeling had greatly abated because the Poles had aligned themselves with the Habsburgs against the Czechs. In *Vanda* Dvořák reverted to certain Wagnerian tendencies; not only is the opera unduly protracted, it is an affair of unmitigated gloom. The première was a fiasco of the first order, only three further performances were given, and the work is perhaps best ignored.

Dvořák allowed only ten months to elapse after the débâcle of *Vanda* before settling down to his next opera in February 1877. Again he turned to a comic theme of Bohemian rustic life, and for his libretto he used one provided for him by J.O. Veselý, a young medical man of the age of 23. It is a comedy in two acts called the 'Cunning Peasant' (*Šelma sedlák*), and perhaps the best appreciation it is possible to give of it is a quotation from Kurt Honolka: '. . . [Veselý is] a not untalented but megalomaniac young man . . .', '. . . a mixture of *Nozze di Figaro* and the "Bartered Bride" . . .', and later: 'Dvořák was at home in the . . . rural world of unmalicious humour and wasted some of his best music on this operatic attempt'. It had its first performance at the National Theatre on 27 January 1878 and was an initial success, but despite the enthusiastic review it received from the celebrated Czech poet and critic Jan Neruda, and despite the truly Dvořákian music that it contains it could not hold its place in the opera repertoire. However it deserves to be mentioned, as it was the first Dvořák opera to be performed outside Czechoslovakia (in Dresden in 1882 under Ernst Schuch). Indeed it was received with wild enthusiasm at the Dresden première, but the elation abated and the opera was taken out of the repertoire after only four performances. When it was performed in Vienna in 1885 the reception was decidedly negative, for on the sketch at the end of Act I of the Oratorio *Svatá Ludmila* Dvořák wrote very acidly: 'Completed in the days when "The Cunning Peasant" was murdered in Vienna'. Once again a bad libretto proved ruinous for Dvořák's musical outpourings.

The next two operas, *Dimitrij* and *Jacobín* ('The Jacobin'), can be bracketed together for more than one reason. Marie Červinková-Riegrová was the librettist of both, the best librettist Dvořák had had up to date, and they must be considered the first major and stageworthy operas he had produced so far. They were also to be the last operas he composed before his years in America. *Dimitrij* was written in 1881/82, *Jacobín* in 1887/88. *Dimitrij*, an Historic Opera in Four Acts, is a virtual successor to Mussorgsky's *Boris Godunov* and is partially based on Schiller's dramatic fragment *Demetrius*. Dimitrij (Demetrius) believes himself to be the rightful successor to the throne of the Russian Empire after Boris, and the whole opera is as deliciously bloodthirsty as any opera lover could wish for and is a work which has fallen into completely undeserved neglect. *Jacobín* is, however, a superior opera. Here Dvořák goes back to his truly native countryside and the very essence of his personality. In 'Benda' he gives us a portrait of Liehmann, that teacher whom he revered, that kindly schoolmaster-*cum*-organist, and he even went so far as to give Benda's daughter the name of Terinka – the name of Liehmann's own daughter. Also, as has been mentioned before, the palace which provides the stage scenery in *Jacobín* must surely be none other than the Palais Veltrusy. Both operas had their first performance in the National Theatre in Prague – *Dimitrij* in 1885, and *Jacobín* in 1889 – and were enthusiastically received. By 1892, *Dimitrij* had had fifty performances and had also been presented in Vienna, and *Jacobín* had 34 performances during the first five years of its existence. Both operas have remained firm favourites with the Czech audiences but have had little success outside the confines of their native land.

It is in this period that Dvořák had to come to a momentous decision. He was being pressurized by his publisher Simrock, by Hanslick, as well as by directors of various opera houses abroad – especially Vienna – that he should compose operas of a more 'international' nature, not so closely tied to the Bohemian soil. It must have been a difficult decision for him to reach, and this inward struggle is reflected in a number of his works of that time, but in the end he stuck to his guns. It is true that during his years in America Mrs. Jeanette Thurber (of whom more will be said later) interested him in Longfellow's poem *Hiawatha*, and he even made sketches for an opera on the subject. But no suitable libretto could be found, and in the event he used some of those sketches in his last and most popular symphony, 'From the New World'.

The last three operas date from the final decade of his life, those years after his return from America, which he spent almost entirely in Bohemia and during which, strangely, he reverted to Wagner and the Neo-German school in general. They are 'The Devil and Kate' (*Čert a Káča*, composed 1898/99), *Rusalka* (composed 1900) and *Armida* (composed 1902/03), but it must also be mentioned that eight days after completing *Armida* he started toying with another operatic project, *Horymír*, to a libretto by Rudolf Stárek. In Vysoká, Dvořák had always been on friendly terms with the miners of Příbram and had shown great sympathy with their strenuous life. Part of this opera was to be set in the mines, complete with authentic mining machinery and, according to the reminiscences of his son Otakar, he promised the miners that at the première he would reserve the whole auditorium of the National Theatre for them so that they might give their opinion. However, the project never got beyond a few preliminary sketches.

In considering Dvořák's last three operas let us first deal with *Armida*, on which he spent the last eighteen months or so of his working life. Why, for the first time since *Alfred*, he was to abandon that field of national history and folklore to which he had devoted all his life's energies, is difficult to fathom. After all, there are many operas by other composers on the subject of Armida (by Lully, Gluck and Haydn among others). The action takes place in Syria during the time of the crusades – an environment and era completely alien to Dvořák. It is a *Grand Opera* effort in four acts, and perhaps he thought – but by now too late – that he could make an operatic success in the international sphere by choosing a non-Slav subject. But he

himself considered Vrchlický's libretto, based on Torquato
Tasso's *La Gerusalemme liberata*, worthy enough to spend a
full year and a half on it. When the opera came to be put into
rehearsals at the National Theatre in November 1903, *Armida*
was dogged by bad luck from the very beginning: everybody
was at loggerheads with everybody else – composer, librettist,
conductor, producer – and the première (under the apparently
very mediocre direction of František Picka) on 25 March 1904
was poorly received. After only seven performances *Armida*
was discarded and was not revived at the National Theatre
until 1928. Abroad it had its first presentation in Bremen in
1961 in a revised version by Kurt Honolka, and nowadays it is
only brought out of a dusty cupboard for commemorative
occasions, even in Czechoslovakia.

This leaves us with the two works which I have no hesitation
in declaring Dvořák's masterpieces in the operatic field; 'The
Devil and Kate' and *Rusalka*. The former is a rumbustious
comedy with a libretto by Adolf Wenig, based on a play by J.K.
Tyl who, in turn, took the story element from a well-known
Bohemian fairy-tale. It is a fitting counterpart to Shakespeare's
Taming of the Shrew (please note both heroines have the
same name!) except that here Kate does *not* get tamed, but
gets the better of that nitwit of a devil Marbuel. The first
performance took place in Prague in 1899 under Adolf Čech
and was a tremendous success – indeed in the following year
Dvořák was awarded the first prize of 2000 Kronen by the
Czech Academy of Sciences and Arts for this opera. Why this
work has not found a place in the repertoire side by side with
Humperdinck's *Hänsel und Gretel* as a Christmas enter-
tainment for children, and as a first introduction of the young
to the medium of opera, is beyond my understanding.

Rusalka is a different matter. The librettist Jaroslav Kvapil
later wrote in an article:

'In the autumn of the year 1899, when I wrote the libretto
Rusalka, I had no idea that I was writing it for Antonín
Dvořák. I wrote it not knowing for whom . . . It is true that

my secret wish was that it might come to Dvořák's notice, but I did not dare to approach him . . .'.*

He had previously shown it to Suk, Nedbal and Foerster, who all turned it down. Dvořák was delighted with it, and Kvapil was overjoyed. The plot is based on the story of *Undine*, a subject which had already been treated by E.T.A. Hoffmann and Lortzing as well as by Weber (although in the latter's *Silvana* it was a spirit of the forest and not a water sprite). It is an ancient story of a human falling in love with a being from another world. The story is heart-rending, and so is the music. Throughout, Dvořák's admiration for Wagner is revealed. The dryads do remind one of the Rhine Maidens in the *Ring*, and the Water Goblin Vodník seems to be a sort of benign though somewhat ineffectual Alberich, but on the whole the opera must be recognized as a masterpiece – dramatic, deeply-felt, organic. The witch Ježibaba is in no way terrifying, and the humorous exchanges between the Gamekeeper and the Turnspit are worthy parallels to the light interludes which Shakespeare provides in his tragedies.

Rusalka had its first performance at the National Theatre in March 1901, and the first night was a triumph such as Dvořák had never witnessed in the opera house before. How thrilled he was can best be seen if we quote his librettist Kvapil:

'. . .First thing in the morning after the première, Dvořák called in to us at the Theatre office in the best of moods. Straight away on seeing me, he calls out: "And now, quick, quick, a new libretto!" I reply: "I haven't any, Master." And he: "Then write something quick as long as I feel like it" . . . I promised. Yes, I promised. But I did not keep my word.'

Rusalka is the only Dvořák opera which, so far, has made its mark internationally. In more recent times Kurt Honolka – the

---

*This quote (as well as many subsequent excerpts) is taken from *Antonín Dvořák, Letters and Reminiscences*, ed. Otakar Šourek (Artia, Prague 1954).

Bohemian-born musician, musicologist, writer and critic, now resident in Germany – has made valiant efforts to further their progress by re-writing and improving the German texts of operas like 'The Cunning Peasant', *Dimitrij, Jacobín,* 'The Devil and Kate' and *Armida,* and all have had their success, albeit only short-lived. May opera houses and the powers-that-be begin to wake up to the beauties they – and their public – are missing by this neglect of Dvořák's operatic output.

THE TURN OF THE TIDE

The years 1871-73 represent a major turning point in Dvořák's personal as well as his professional life. He formed two new friendships which were to have great bearing on much of what was to follow. The first of these was with Dr. Ludevít Procházka, a lawyer, and his wife Marta, herself a singer. Theirs was a music-loving home, and it was at their soirées that some of Dvořák's music – songs and some chamber music – was first performed. Procházka took a great interest in Dvořák and furthered him as best he could, and it was probably due to Procházka that, in 1873, the first of Dvořák's compositions saw the light of day in print, published by Starý of Prague: a cycle of six songs, and a Potpourri for Piano from the opera 'King and Charcoal Burner' (Version I). Whether or not the Procházkas influenced Dvořák in any way when he made the decision to resign from the orchestra of the National Theatre in July 1871 in order to devote more time to composition will always remain a matter of conjecture. The other friendship which he formed during those important years was with the merchant Jan Neff and his wife, who asked him to become the piano teacher of their two children in January 1873.

In March or April 1872 Dvořák began work on what must be considered his first important composition: a *Hymnus* with the subtitle 'The Heirs of the White Mountain' (*Dědicové Bílé Hory*) for chorus and orchestra on a text by Vítězslav Hálek. The dead heroes of the battle of the White Mountain – where the fate of Bohemia was sealed in 1620 – play as important a part in Bohemian folklore as do the warriors of the earlier Hussite Wars and are a symbol of fervent Czech patriotism and resistance. The subject must have been very near and dear to Dvořák's heart: he gave full vent to his national feelings, and in consequence his Wagnerian leanings receded into the background. In later years (1880 and 1884) he revised the work, and eventually it was published by Novello in 1885, but the most important thing is that his friend Karel Bendl gave the first performance on 9 March 1873 with the Prague Hlahol Choral Society. It was a great success, it represented the breakthrough for Dvořák, and the Prague musical circles began to realize that his was a name to be reckoned with. It is worth noting that this first success occured when Dvořák was 31 – the age at which Schubert died.

In his personal life the year 1873 must have stood out for ever after. Having been jilted by Josefina and having courted Anna for years, he had always met with the obstruction of her father, Jan Čermák: a penniless musician just was no match for the daughter of a well-to-do goldsmith. But in February 1873 Čermák died, one month later Dvořák had the great success with his *Hymnus*, one of his songs was published, and Slánský conducted one of his three Nocturnes ('May Night'), so ultimately mother Klotilda Čermáková gave her consent to the marriage between Antonín and her daughter Anna. The fact that their first child was born less than five months after that event may also have had some bearing on the matter. Whether the date of their wedding was chosen on purpose, or whether it was just one of those coincidences we do not know, but the fact remains that they were married on 17 November 1873, 33 years to the day after the wedding of Dvořák's own parents. (To jump ahead – and this time it surely was by design – their daughter Otilie married the composer Josef Suk on the day of their Silver Wedding Anniversary, on 17 November

1898). For the first months of their married life they lived with
Anna's mother, and it was there that their first child, Otakar
(I), was born on 4 April 1874. Then, in May 1874, the young
couple with their baby son moved into a flat in Na Rybníčku
No. 14. It was the first time in his life that Dvořák could call a
home his own.

By all accounts Anna must have been the ideal wife for
Dvořák and a devoted mother to their nine children. But she
must also have had a shrewd and business-like brain for,
although we have no direct evidence, it seems likely that in his
dealings with publishers, agents and the like she was a sort of
spiritus movens when it came to drawing up contracts and
generally getting down to money matters.

Shortly after his marriage, in February 1874 and possibly at
the instigation of Anna, Dvořák applied for and obtained the
position of organist at St. Adalbert's Church (*sv. Vojtěch*)
where his former teacher Josef Foerster was in charge of the
choir. He, incidentally, was also the father of Dvořák's friend
Josef Bohuslav who later became a composer of considerable
importance in Czech music. At St. Adalbert's Dvořák earned
the princely salary of 126 Gulden* per annum, and he fulfilled
his duties there for precisely three years until he resigned in
February 1877. Needless to say, he had to continue to
supplement his income by doing as much teaching as possible
and also some viola playing, but even so the financial resources
must have been pretty scant, a situation which did not change
until he won the Austrian State Grant.

It is obvious that one can only understand Dvořák's music if
one also understands his basic character as well as his attitude

*In order to give the reader some idea as to monetary values in those days,
the following information obtained by courtesy of the Cabinet Office
(Central Statistical Office), the Bank of England, and other sources may be
of interest. In the 1880s the rate of exchange was approx. 12.5 Gulden to the
£. Between 1885 and 1983, the U.K. Retail Price Index (based on January
1974 =100) rose from 13.2 to 336.5. This would imply that, in terms of buying
power, Dvořák's annual salary at St. Adalbert's was in the region of £257.00
p.a. by todays' standards.

to life in general and the world around him. That he was a devout Roman Catholic has already been said. His religion was a matter of course to him: he believed in it, he acted by it and its precepts, but he never made a particular show of it. However, at the end of most of his scores, particularly major works, we find his autograph comments *Bohu díky* ('Thanks to God'), *Chvála Bohu* ('Praised be the Lord') or *Zaplať pán Bůh* ('God will repay you'). To this must be added his great love for nature. He was a very early riser and usually began his day with a walk. In Prague he had to content himself with the trees and birds in Karlovo Náměsti (Charles Square), but in later years, in Vysoká and also during his American summer holiday in Spillville, he really could roam the countryside This deep feeling of communion with nature is never far absent from all his music. Hans Gál once said to me that Dvořák was 'a composer who worked in his shirt sleeves'. Of course Gál said these words thinking of the music, but they also have an appliction in a much more literal sense. It is undoubtedly due to his family background and upbringing that there was nothing swanky about him. Throughout his life, even when he had become famous, he always remained a somewhat staid, taciturn, middle-class citizen who liked to go to bed early, disliked official and ostentatious occasions, receptions and the like and hated being treated with obsequiousness. This is perhaps best exemplified by the reply he gave in 1886 to a choral conductor who had written to him in terms of utmost flattery:

'I must confess quite frankly that your kind letter has embarrassed me somewhat. The reason is its excessive adulation and devotion, for this looks as though you were speaking to a demi-God which I never have considered, do not consider, and never shall consider myself to be. I am just a simple Bohemian musician who does not like such exaggerated servilities, and although I have moved about enough in the great world of music, I shall still remain what I always have been – a simple Bohemian musician . . .'

His basic joys were modest. Apart from his two great hobbies – locomotives and pigeons – he was happiest when he spent a few hours in the circle of his friends in some coffee house or other, drinking beer, smoking a cigar, and chatting generally. Later on another pastime was added to these unpretentious pleasures: playing skittles.

But next to his music the dominant factor in his life was his family. He was the ideal husband and father to whom family and other festivities meant the world, particularly Christmas, and he generally made a point of never working on Christmas Day. This feeling of one-ness becomes especially apparent in the letters he wrote home during the years when he was in America. When at home, as early as the days in Na Rybníčku – and here we come back to this 'composing in shirt sleeves' – he loved working in the kitchen, despite the household noises, with the kids probably making quite a din and banging saucepan lids. Apparently noise did not distract him in the least, as long as the noise was *un*musical, but if someone was practising the piano or some other instrument of definite pitch within earshot, this would put him off completely. Perhaps this was also one of the reasons why he decided to leave the Na Rybníčku (where the living quarters were somewhat cramped in any case) in November 1877 and take a flat in the Žitná.

What is also relevant at this juncture is to take a look at his compositions of those years, again only going into detail as far as the more important works are concerned. During the time when he was busy on his *Hymnus* in 1872 nothing else was allowed to interfere, but in the second half of that year he got down to other compositions again: two cycles of songs, three Nocturnes for orchestra (of which only the second, 'May Night', has remained extant), and it was probably also at this time that he wrote the Silhouettes for piano which, however, were only cast into their final form in which we know them nowadays in 1879. But the only composition of some importance is the Piano Quintet in A (op. 5) which he wrote in

August 1872. Its main claim to fame lies in the fact that the
Procházkas organized a matinée for it to be performed on 22
November 1872, engaging a fine team of musicians to give
Dvořák the best possible opportunity, and this was the first
time that one of his chamber music works was heard in public.
Dvořák was dissatisfied with the work. First he discarded it
completely, but in later years he revised it, making drastic (and
very necessary) cuts. In the end, however, he was still unhappy
with this 'paste-and-scissors' job, and immediately after this
attempted revision he settled down, in 1887, to write that great
Piano Quintet in A (op. 81) which is so well known and must be
considered one of the finest chamber music works he ever
produced.

Almost eight years had passed since the completion of
Symphony No. 2, and Dvořák felt ready to try this form again.
Between April and July 1873 he wrote his Symphony No. 3 in E
flat which is his only symphony in three movements. The work
shows clearly Dvořák's departure from Wagnerianism.
Possibly it was the breakthrough of the *Hymnus* which gave
him the impetus to embark on a work of major proportions
again, and this symphony certainly stands head and shoulders
above its two predecessors. The first movement is unmistak-
able Dvořák, and even someone who has never heard the
work before and does not know what he is listening to will
surely recognize Dvořák from the very first melody – a melody
with that broad sweep which became such a characteristic in
so many of his later works. Here he finds himself to be
sufficiently a master to relax the absolute strictness of sonata
form and allow himself more personal freedom. The
movement is also much more concise than in either of his
earlier symphonies, and never before had Dvořák allowed his
love for the *Furiant* to become so incisive – a trait which was to
recur in many of his later compositions. It is only in the second
movement that Wagner rears his head again, for it is
impossible not to think of the Master of Bayreuth when
listening to the central section, but then follows a Finale which,
at the very outset, shows all the signs of having a true Finale

character. Unfortunately the dotted rhythm which at first gives the movement so much impetus and spice becomes somewhat monotonously repetitive.

The only other works which bear mention from that year 1873 are the String Quartets No. 5 in F minor and No. 6 in A minor. Unfortunately their original manuscripts are not completely handed down to us, but we know enough about them to form a clear opinion that, although Dvořák still tended to long-windedness and although certain influences of the Neo-German school persisted, he had become much more concise and concentrated in his thematic material. The Neo-German influence is most pronounced in the fact that he originally conceived the A minor Quartet as a work in one continuous movement though in five linked sections, but later he separated these and turned it into a quartet in the customary four movements. Perhaps the most important aspect of these string quartets is that later he isolated the second movement of the F minor Quartet and re-wrote it as a Romance for violin with either piano or orchestral accompaniment, and this has probably become the best-known music from the two quartets. He dedicated it to František Ondříček who, ten years later, was to be the soloist in the first performance of the Violin Concerto. It is a charming, unpretentious work, and should be heard more often, but unfortunately it is too short to be programmed easily in public concerts. However, like certain other small-scale compositions in Dvořák's *oeuvre*, it has proved very useful to gramophone companies as a 'filler'. Also in 1873 he composed an Octet and an overture 'Romeo and Juliet', both of which are listed by him amongst the works which he himself had destroyed, and they are no longer extant. Nevertheless the Overture at least may have some bearing on the subject of his application for the Austrian State Grant.

With the advent of 1874 Dvořák appears to have turned over a new leaf – indeed, on New Year's Day of that year he began with the composition of his Symphony No. 4 in D minor, and it gives the impression that he had decided to abandon his experimental ideas to some extent and follow more strictly along the lines of classic formal principles. The first movement has a cohesion yet freedom similar to that of the first movement of its predecessor. Then Wagner appears again in the second movement: from the beginning it inevitably conjures up visions of the *Tannhäuser* pilgrims marching along in the mid-distance; in his symphonic output this was, however, to be the last time Dvořák was so blatantly Wagnerian. Then we are more than rewarded by a Scherzo and Trio which are utterly Bohemian. In the Trio I am irresistibly reminded of a typical band of itinerant Bohemian musicians! In the last movement, once again, Dvořák wrestled – not quite successfully – with the Finale problem, one with which most composers from the *Eroica* onwards up to Gustav Mahler and symphonists of the 20th century had to wrestle, and few have solved it convincingly. There is one feature of Dvořák's music, inaugurated in this symphony, which seems to me to have been overlooked: an innate feeling for the 'cantering rhythm' so prevalent in the music of Bohemian composers. It occurs frequently in Schubert, particularly in the Finale of his great C major Symphony (and let us not forget that Schubert, the epitome of Viennese music, had parents who were born in Moravia and Bohemian Silesia respectively) and we often find it in Smetana, especially in *Šarka*. In Dvořák it first comes to the fore in this D minor Symphony, in a most pronounced manner in the Scherzo, where this 'cantering rhythm' accompanies an undiluted Bohemian tune, and we are to find it again very strongly in his last two symphonies. He completed the composition on 25 March 1874, and only a few days later Smetana gave the first performance of the Symphony No. 3 in a Philharmonic Concert. It was the first of Dvořák's symphonies to be played in public, and less than two months afterwards Smetana also conducted the Scherzo from the new Symphony No. 4 – the complete work was first heard under Dvořák's own direction in 1892. All of this must have filled him with great pride and joy. Generally speaking we can say that the first two symphonies must be considered early attempts which betray much immaturity, whereas No. 3 and No. 4 represent the transitional stage before we come to the five mature ones. No. 3 and No. 4 were published by Simrock as late as 1911/12 with the designation *Aus dem Nachlass* ('op. posth.').

Let us just mention briefly that, less than a month after completing the Symphony No. 4, he settled down to the second version of his 'King and Charcoal Burner', and it took him almost seven months to get this off his chest – seven precious months wasted in a lost cause, and he spent some more time on this non-starter in 1897. However, he had the satisfaction that this second version was staged by the National Theatre, and that the Potpourri for Piano which he concocted from it was published by Wetzler of Prague in 1875.

While still at work on the last stages of the second version of 'King and Charcoal Burner', Dvořák composed two more instrumental works: a Rhapsody in A minor (op. 14) which he later re-named 'Symphonic Poem' and which was neither performed nor published until after his death, and his String Quartet No. 7 in A minor (op. 16) which was to be the first chamber music work of his to be published, again by Starý, in 1875. The rest of that year 1874, from about September until Christmas Eve, was completely taken up with the composition of his one-act opera 'The -Stubborn Lovers'.

At that time the Ministry of Education in Vienna awarded an annual Austrian State Grant to 'young, poor and talented artists', and by now Dvořák felt sure enough of himself to apply for such a Grant. The prerequisite was to prove that he was a musician and without means, all of which was officially attested by 'The Town Clerk's Office of the Royal Capital of Prague'. Then, some time in July 1874, Dvořák made his official application, at the same time submitting a number of scores. It has generally been believed that the works he submitted were his two last symphonies, No. 3 and No. 4, together with a chamber music work. (Some authorities claim that the symphonies were No. 2 and No. 3, and they all differ as to which chamber music work he sent.) However, the latest research on the part of John Clapham has brought to light a report of the Minister, Karl Stremayer, which states that Dvořák had

> ' . . . submitted fifteen compositions, among them symphonies and overtures for full orchestra which display an undoubted talent, but in a way which as yet remains formless and unbridled. This talent is shown in a much purer and more pleasing manner in Dvořák's pictures [songs] from the "Dvůr Kralové Manuscript", which display genuine and original gifts . . .'

There is no record as to what scores he saw fit to offer, but one can assume that the symphonies were indeed No. 3 and No. 4, and that he had at that time not yet destroyed the 'Romeo and Juliet' overture, as otherwise it could only have been those to *Alfred* and 'King and Charcoal Burner'. For the rest of it, all is conjecture.

The jury in Vienna consisted of the Director of the Vienna *Hofoper*, Johann Herbeck, the famous music critic Eduard Hanslick, and Johannes Brahms. They unanimously awarded him the scholarship in January 1875, and in February Dvořák was the proud and happy recipient of 400 Gulden (about £815 in terms of present-day buying power, cf. footnote page 56), probably the largest lump sum of money that so far he had ever had in all his life, and badly needed in his financial circumstances. It was not the only time that he was to receive this Grant: he applied for it again in the following years, and according to Šourek he was successful 'five years in succession', whereas according to Clapham he only received the Grant again on the strength of his third and fourth applications. But, useful – and, indeed, essential – as those 400 Gulden must have been for Dvořák in that February 1875, another aspect is of far greater importance: it brought him to the notice of Brahms who was to have such a tremendous influence on his future career, and who was later to become such a staunch and loyal friend.

INTERLUDIUM II:
DVOŘÁK – BRAHMS – SIMROCK

Brahms and Dvořák – a somewhat incongruous pair. On the one hand we have Brahms, the North German Protestant and Freethinker, a city-dweller born and bred, well read with a strong interest in philosophical matters, and a confirmed bachelor – on the other there is Dvořák, that devoutly Roman Catholic Bohemian, a child of nature, with only a few leanings towards literature and philosophy, and a model family man, husband, and father. Yet for a period spanning nearly twenty years right up to Brahms' death in 1897 these two composers were the closest of friends, and there can hardly be a parallel in the entire history of music to the generosity and assistance which Brahms – Dvořák's senior by eight years – extended to his younger colleague at all times. Indeed, it would be no exaggeration to say that, without Brahms' help, Dvořák could not have achieved all he *did* achieve.

As we have just seen, Brahms was on the jury which awarded the annual State Grant which the Austrian Government gave to young and deserving artists, and it was in 1874 – when Dvořák applied for this Grant for the first time – that he attracted Brahms' attention. However, there was no direct communication between the two men until Dvořák wrote to Brahms towards the end of 1877, and there is no better way of outlining the relationship between them during those early stages than by quoting from their correspondence, including Brahms' letters to Simrock, his own publisher in Berlin and one of the leading music publishers of the day.

Dvořák to Brahms on 3 December 1877:

'. . . At the suggestion of the esteemed Prof. Hanslick I venture to address these few lines to you, honoured Master, in order to express to you my deep-felt thanks for the kindness you have shown me.

What I count a still greater happiness, however, is the sympathy you have been good enough to accord to my modest talent and the favour with which (as Prof. Hanslick tells me) you received my Czech vocal duets [the Moravian Duets]. Prof. Hanslick now advises me to procure a German translation of these songs which you, dear Sir, would be so kind as to recommend to your publishers. It is my duty to address myself to you with one more request – that you should be good enough to be of assistance to me in this matter which, for me, is of such great importance. It would be, indeed, not only for me but also for my beloved country, of immeasurable value if you, honoured Master, whose works delight in such great measure the whole musical world, would give me such an introduction.

With the earnest request that I may continue in the future to enjoy your highly valued favour, I beg your kind permission to forward to you for your inspection some of my chamber music works and compositions for orchestra. . . .'

Brahms replied shortly afterwards in that same December. The letter is undated:

'. . . Allow me quite shortly to thank you for your lines and for the great pleasure I have derived from the works you sent me. I have taken the liberty of writing about them, and especially about the "Duets", to Mr. Fritz Simrock. . . .

From the title it would appear that the Duets are still

your property, in which case you could sell them to Mr. Simrock. The only thing that is needed is to get a good German translation. Can you manage that? In any case I beg you not to rush the matter so that the work may not suffer in consequence. In the meantime you could perhaps send the folio to Mr. Simrock to have a look at? The rest will then follow. . . .'

That Brahms was as good as his word is shown by the recommendation which he wrote to Simrock on 12 December 1877:

'Dear S.

In connection with the State Grant I have for several years past had great pleasure in the works of Antonín Dvořák (pronounced Dworschak) in Prague. This year he sent in, among other things, a volume (10) of "Duets for two sopranos with piano accompaniment" [sic – actually they were written for soprano and alto], which seems to be very suitable and practical for publication. . . . Dvořák has written all sorts of things, operas (Czech), symphonies, quartets and piano music. There is no doubt he is very talented. And then he is also poor. I beg you to think the matter over. The "Duets" won't give you much thought and will possibly sell well. . . .'

To Brahms' earlier letter, Dvořák replied on 19 December 1877, expressing his gratitude, telling him that he had sent the Duets with a German translation to Simrock, and at the same time he also enclosed a copy of that German translation with his letter to Brahms for his approval. Simrock, in the event, published the Duets (the second and third of the four cycles of Moravian Duets that Dvořák wrote) in 1878 as op.32 under the title *Klänge aus Mähren*, and they caught on like wildfire. Thus began a business connection between Dvořák and Simrock which soon blossomed into friendship, but later (as we shall see) frictions arose, and the friendship turned into something of a love-hate relationship. For the Moravian Duets Dvořák did not receive a penny, but this did not greatly perturb him:

the all-important thing was that he now had music published in Germany, and thereby his name became known beyond the confines of Prague and the Czech Lands.

Some time in December 1877 (we do not know the exact date, but it must certainly have been after 21 December) Dvořák travelled to Vienna in order to meet Brahms and thank him personally but, alas, Brahms was away on a concert tour, so he could only call on Eduard Hanslick, with whom he established cordial relations. So, on 23 January 1878, Dvořák wrote to Brahms again, bringing him up to date with his dealings with Simrock, and then continuing:

'. . . And now I venture, highly honoured Master, to approach you with a request. Permit me, out of gratitude and a deep respect for your incomparable musical works, to offer you the dedication of my D minor Quartet.

It would be for me the highest honour I can aspire to and I should be the happiest of men to have the honour to subscribe myself as bound to you in eternal gratitude. . . .'

It is worthwhile to quote Brahms' reply (of March 1878) in full, for it throws so much light on the warm-hearted character of Brahms the Man:

'I regret extremely that I was away from home when you were here. The more so as I have such an aversion to letter-writing that I cannot hope to make up for it in the least by correspondence. And, today, no more than to say that to occupy myself with your things gives me the greatest pleasure, but that I would give a good deal to be able to discuss individual points with you personally. You write somewhat hurriedly. When you are filling in the numerous missing sharps, flats and naturals, then it would be good to look a little more closely at the notes themselves and at the voice parts, etc.

Forgive me, but it is very desirable to point out such things to a man like you. I also accept the works just as they are very gratefully and consider myself honoured by the dedication of the quartet.

I think it would be very good if you gave me both the quartets that I know. If Simrock should not be willing, might I try to place them elsewhere? . . .'

Shortly after writing this letter, just before setting off on a holiday, on 5 April 1878, Brahms gave Simrock yet another little prod regarding Dvořák:

'. . .I don't know what further risk you are wanting to take with this man. I have no idea about business or what interest there is for larger works. I do not care to make recommendations, because I have only my eyes and my ears and they are altogether my own. If you should think of going on with it at all, get him to send you his two string quartets, major and minor, and have them played to you. The best that a musician can have *Dvořák has*, and it is in these compositions. . . .'

In November 1878 Dvořák travelled to Berlin for the first time in his life to make the personal acquaintance of Fritz Simrock, but it was not until he went to Vienna a month later that he first met Brahms face to face. The two men must have understood each other perfectly from the very moment they met, for musically and humanly they were on common ground, even though in other respects they were poles apart. In this connection it is perhaps worth citing a passage from Josef Suk's *Aus meiner Jugend*, memoirs from the days of his youth. In March 1896 Anna and Antonín Dvořák were in Vienna in the company of their future son-in-law, Suk, and called on Brahms. Suk writes:

'. . .it is a visit I shall never forget. Brahms tried to persuade Dvořák to move to Vienna and because he knew that he had a big family, he said: "Look here, Dvořák, you have a lot of children and I have almost nobody. If you need anything, my fortune is at your disposal." The tears came into Mrs. Dvořák's eyes and Dvořák, deeply touched, seized the Master's hand. Then the conversation turned to faith and religion. . . . On the way back to the hotel, Dvořák was more than usually silent. At last after some considerable time he exclaimed: "Such a man, such a soul – and he doesn't believe in anything, he doesn't believe in anything!" . . .'

Both Brahms and Simrock very soon returned the visits and came to see Dvořák in Prague, Brahms in January 1879 and Simrock in March. Not many details are known, but both continued their efforts to further the cause of Dvořák, Simrock presumably for business reasons, but Brahms out of pure altruistic friendship. It was probably Simrock who drew the attention of Louis Ehlert, one of Germany's most influential music critics, to Dvořák's music, and Ehlert remained one of Dvořák's staunchest supporters to his dying day. Through Brahms, directly or indirectly, Dvořák came in contact with Joseph Joachim, Hellmesberger, Hans Richter and, later, Hans von Bülow, all of whom became enthusiastic protagonists of his music and performed it wherever they could.

From now on the correspondence between Dvořák and Brahms becomes somewhat sporadic, but they met whenever possible, and their friendship suffered no break. It seems that in October 1883 Dvořák specially went to Vienna to visit Brahms, and afterwards he wrote enthusiastically to Simrock:

'. . .I have never seen him in such a happy mood. We were together every noon and evening, and had much to talk about. He seems to take pleasure in my company and I am so captivated by his kindness both as an artist and as a man that I can find it in my heart to love him. . . . You know how reserved he is as regards his creative work even towards his dearest friends, but he has never been so with me. My wish to hear something from his new Symphony [No. 3 in F] he granted at once and played the first and last movements. . . .'

Dvořák saw Brahms for the last time in March 1897, when Brahms was already desperately ill, and on his return he wrote to Simrock: '. . . I was in Vienna and visited Master Brahms, and saw how true, unfortunately, is all I heard from you. Nevertheless let us hope that all is not yet lost! God grant it may be so!...' However, that hope was not to be fulfilled. Brahms died on 3 April 1897, and a matter of three weeks after his March visit Dvořák was back in Vienna to attend the funeral of his great friend and benefactor on 6 April.

The relations with Simrock were not allowed to run such an unruffled course. For one thing, unlike Brahms, he was a business man, and a pretty shrewd one at that, and for another he had little sympathy and understanding for Dvořák's nationalistic feelings. At first things went smoothly: the Moravian Duets proved to be a success, and he got them for nothing. It is also true that, once they got to know each other personally, Simrock and Dvořák were on exceedingly friendly terms which went so far that in some of his letters Dvořák addressed Simrock by the Czech pet name 'Dear Fricku' and signed himself similarly 'Your Tonda'. But the main thing is that Simrock had begun to realize that with Dvořák he was onto a good thing. Brahms' Hungarian Dances had also proved a good thing, and so Simrock had the bright idea of suggesting to Dvořák that he should write something along the same lines. The result was the first set of Slavonic Dances which, like his model Brahms, Dvořák first wrote for piano duet and later orchestrated. Simrock was delighted and published the piano duet version without paying Dvořák anything. However, during the same year 1878 he also published them in their orchestral setting and paid Dvořák all of 300 Marks for them. They caught on everywhere, and it is impossible to estimate how much of a fortune he himself earned with these dances, but Dvořák proudly showed those 300 Marks to all his friends: they were the first publisher's fee he had earned. Nevertheless it is gratifying to know that when it came to the second set of Slavonic Dances in 1886/87, Simrock had to stump up ten times that amount.

During the years that followed they exchanged a large

number of letters, mainly concerned with professional matters, and they also met twice – in May 1881 and May 1882 – in Carlsbad (now Karlovy Vary) with Hanslick being there also. The first frictions arose over the spelling of Dvořák's name in the printed editions: Dvořák insisted on the Czech spelling 'Antonín' of his Christian name, whereas Simrock simply wanted to put the German form 'Anton'. After a certain amount of wrangling they reached a compromise, and in future Dvořák's Christian name simply appeared in the abbreviated form of 'Ant.', which satisfied both parties.

The second bone of contention also concerned the question of the Czech language. Simrock wanted to publish Dvořák's works with German titles only, but Dvořák had a deep-rooted aversion to the German language and only made use of it when there was no alternative. He insisted that on his published works the titles should appear in both German and Czech, but this is a point which he only won a good few years later.

Another thing which annoyed Dvořák, particularly in later years, was the fact that Simrock took to altering his opus numbers. Once Dvořák was an established name, Simrock started to take an interest in Dvořák's earlier compositions and published many of them, but in order to give the impression that they were recent works he gave some of them higher opus numbers than corresponded to the facts. This may have been sharp business practise, and Dvořák's annoyance is understandable. But on the other hand, he himself also did a bit of cheating, possibly at Anna's instigation. In 1879 he had made a verbal agreement that Simrock should have first option on anything new which Dvořák composed; however, he still had certain moral obligations to other publishers such as Bote & Bock, Hofmeister,* and Schlesinger, and some of them paid better than Simrock. So he resorted to the subterfuge of giving certain of his works artificially low opus numbers to make it appear that they had been composed before he made this agreement with Simrock. Quite apart

*Hofmeister of Leipzig – not to be confused with the Viennese publisher Hoffmeister!

from the fact that the ethical aspect of this procedure is
somewhat dubious, it also served to increase still further the
unholy muddle regarding the opus numbers of Dvořák's
works.

Nevertheless they remained on reasonably cordial terms,
and in early 1885 Dvořák reported to Simrock in a humorous
vein '. . . that there is a new opus in our family – a boy [Otakar
(II)]! So you see, a new symphony [No. 7, D minor] and a boy in
addition! What do you say to this creative strength? . . .' But
the successes which Dvořák had reaped in England during the
preceding year had reinforced his self-esteem, and he had also
found that there were English publishers who were only too
eager to publish his music. Simrock had been nagging him for
some time that there was no money in publishing large scale
works; he wanted more dances, songs, small works for piano
and the like. In addition, Simrock was apt to be somewhat
tight-fisted when it came to fees. The whole situation is
perhaps best summed up by a letter which Dvořák wrote on 18
May 1885 in reply to a letter from Simrock, who had offered
3000 Marks for the D minor Symphony:

'. . . I fully recognize the validity of the points you put
forward, that is, from the business point of view. I, again,
from mine, must draw attention to important considerations, which I am sure you will also respect.

1. If I give you the Symphony for 3000 M, then I have as
good as lost 3000 M – because another firm offers me this
sum – in which case I should be extremely sorry if you
should wish to force me, so to speak, into such a
situation.

2. I think that even though such large works do not
produce the desired financial effect straight away, the
time may come when everything will be amply made up
for, and

3. I beg you to consider that in my Slavonic Dances you
have found a gold mine which cannot be so easily
underrated, and

4. if you take and consider all that you indicated in your last letter from a common-sense point of view, then we reach a very simple conclusion: not to write symphonies and large vocal and instrumental works, but publish here and there some songs, piano pieces or dances and I know not what else: this, as an artist who wants to make his mark, I cannot do.

Yes, my Friend, you see that is how I look upon it from my artistic point of view, and I hope you will appreciate mine as I do yours. This, however, does not lead to any conclusion. If you do not wish, or, rather, if you simply cannot give me these 6000 M, then all talking and writing comes to an end; what difference is it between you and me if you have 3000 M less and I by so much more. Remember, I pray you, that I am a poor artist and the father of a family and do not wrong me. . . .'

The two men met shortly afterwards, in June 1885, in Carlsbad, and again Hanslick was there too. They reached a sort of uneasy truce: Simrock agreed to pay 6000 Marks for the D minor Symphony, but extracted a promise from Dvořák that he would compose a second set of Slavonic Dances for him.

This truce, however, was to be of a short duration. The vexed question of the spelling of Dvořák's name and of the inclusion of titles in Czech cropped up again, and Dvořák wrote somewhat sharply to Simrock on 22 August 1885:

'. . . Do not laugh at my Czech brothers and do not be sorry for me either. What I asked of you was only a wish, and if you cannot fulfil it I am justified in seeing in it a lack of goodwill on your part such as I have not found either among English or French publishers. . . .'

But only a few months later, on 10 September 1885, he tried to pour oil on the troubled waters by writing again to Simrock:

'. . . But what have *we two to do with politics*; let us be glad that we can dedicate our services to art. And let us

hope that nations which possess and represent *art* will
never perish, no matter how small they are. Forgive me
but I only wanted to say to you that an artist has also his
country in which he must have firm faith and for which he
must have an ardent heart. . . .'

As Simrock kept on with his complaints that he had no use for
big works, Dvořák turned to Novello in London, and in the end
– over the years 1885 to 1893 – they published the majority of
Dvořák's large-scale choral works as well as his Symphony
No. 8. It is true that Dvořák fulfilled his promise to compose
the second set of Slavonic Dances for Simrock, but he was
somewhat tardy with the orchestration. This, coupled with the
fact that Simrock had learnt of Dvořák's negotiations with
Novello, led to a letter from Simrock, dated 21 October 1886:

'. . . Now that your Slavonic op.72 [sic] has just come out,
I must tell you again how *very* delighted I am with *these
splendid* pieces. But – there's no help; they must be orchestrated – they simply shout for it!! And, *Donnerwetter!* if
you don't do it yourself soon I shall have to ask somebody
else to – and don't go promising England any more works
– I shall confiscate them!!!'

But the ructions continued steadily and came to a head in 1890
over the question of the publication of Dvořák's Symphony
No. 8. Simrock complained once again that large-scale works
were a financial loss, Dvořák countered this by saying that, if
Simrock would not take any big works, he would feel himself
free to offer them to other publishers, and Simrock then
invoked the verbal agreement of 1879. This infuriated Dvořák,
and he replied in no uncertain terms on 11 October 1890:

'. . . You seem to have a strange sense of logic: I am to
compose and offer everything to you – and you just turn it
down! . . . Well, I won't be taken for a fool! And if you
start threatening me, then my future demands will
increase considerably . . .'

After this, there was no further communication between Dvořák and Simrock for more than a year.

In the end it was Simrock who renewed the contact in November 1891 after he had come to hear of the success of the *Dumky* Trio, of Dvořák's appointment as Director of the National Conservatory in New York, and of the fact that he was working on a triptych of three overtures. But by then Dvořák was self-assured enough not to allow himself to be wooed so easily and replied that 'there was no hurry'. Dvořák reported the matter to his friend Göbl on 25 November 1891:

'. . . Simrock has remembered my existence, he was probably sorry at not having heard anything about me for so long. He would like to have something again but I am letting him wait in the meantime to punish him. If he doesn't pay me very well, I shan't give him either the "Overtures" or the "Dumky". I shall always be able to get them accepted. I won't allow myself to be done by him any more! – – – . . .'

However, in the summer of 1893 while on his American holiday in Spillville, he relented and wrote to Simrock on 28 July:

'Dear Simrock,

I am spending my four months' holiday here in Spillville, a completely Czech place in the State of Iowa, 1300 miles from New York, with my whole family, where I am very happy, and where I also got your letters. Dear Friend, I am composing now, thank goodness, only for my pleasure. I am fairly independent, have a salary of 15,000 dollars (or 60,000 M) – and so am able to devote my leisure to composing and am content. I am, therefore, in no hurry to publish my works. If you recollect our correspondence in Prague two years ago, you will easily understand why I am holding off publishing my works. In the meantime their number has been added to (by fairly large works) and I shall tell you once more what I have. . . .'

He then proceeded to offer Simrock what we would now call a 'package deal': the *Dumky* Trio, the three Overtures, the 'New World' Symphony, the String Quartet in F plus some smaller works for the sum of 7500 Marks. Simrock accepted, while extracting from Dvořák the promise that in future he, Simrock, would have the sole right to publish all Dvořák's future compositions. Dvořák agreed on condition that Simrock would publish everything which he, Dvořák, composed. It was a 'catch-as-catch-can' arrangement from which both composer and publisher eventually profited, but they both adhered to it. Simrock finally capitulated as far as the Czech titles were concerned, so that Dvořák could be well satisfied with having won a victory. Filled with elation, he wrote to Göbl from New York on 27 February 1894:

> '. . . Perhaps you do not know that I am on good terms again with Simrock. He has bought *everything I had* and *wants all* my new things. . . .'

From now on there was no more tension between composer and publisher. After Dvořák had returned to Czechoslovakia from America in April 1895, he made a point of seeing as many of his old friends as he could. We do not know whether his relationship with Simrock ever became as cordial again as it once had been, but the fact remains that in that year 1895 they met twice in Carlsbad, in May and in August, both times with Hanslick being there as well. The collaboration between the two men only came to an end when Simrock died after a severe illness in Lausanne on 20 August 1901.

FULFILMENT

The period between 1875 and 1883 was that in which the fledgling Dvořák left his nest, spread his wings and soared heavenwards. He was now happily married, a proud father, and financially his position had become somewhat more secure, particularly because of the Austrian State Grant. He was gaining a reputation in his own country, and through the assistance of Brahms and Simrock his name also became known beyond the confines of the Czech Lands. In terms of artistic productivity, these years are the most prolific of his life, particularly the first half of that period. Music just seemed to flow from his pen, and now it becomes utterly impossible to draw a dividing line between Dvořák's life and his musical output: the two simply merge into an entity which is inseparable.

On Christmas Eve 1874 he had completed his opera 'The Stubborn Lovers', and some time in January 1875 he began with the composition of a String Quintet in G (op.77) which he completed in March of that year. In Dvořák's life – he was now in his 34th year – it is a work of utmost importance, as are the Piano Trio in B flat (op.21) and the Piano Quartet in D (op.23) which followed shortly afterwards, for these works are a clear indication of the maturity and self-assurance which he had achieved. Was it the new-found domestic happiness, or was it the honour of being considered worthy by men like Brahms, Hanslick and Herbeck to receive the State Grant? We do not know, but the fact remains that these works exude a feeling of security which, in his earlier compositions, we seek for in vain. It is also curious that these three chamber music works happen to divide the canon of his fourteen string quartets into two neat halves: the first seven in order of composition can be termed early and transitional works, whereas the second seven, from Quartet No. 8 onward, are all works which stem from the mind of a masterly and individual composer, even though they are not necessarily of equal stature. We shall see later that a similar coincidence occurs in his symphonic output.

The String Quintet (whose high opus number, incidentally, was due to the fact that Simrock did not publish it until 1888 and wanted to make it appear that it was composed much later than it was) has a number of strange features. For one thing it is written for a rather unusual combination in that it adds a double bass to the normal string quartet instead of the customary second viola or, more rarely, second cello. Originally it was conceived in five movements, the first slow movement, *Andante religioso*, being an adaptation of the second movement of the E minor String Quartet of 1870. Dvořák eventually discarded this movement and re-worked it for string orchestra under the title *Nokturno* (op.40). The Quintet is exuberantly Bohemian, outgoing, and although it is in no way formless, one cannot help feeling that Dvořák had shaken off all shackles which previously had impeded him so much, and was able to give full rein to his imagination and his true self.

During the same months, the first half of the year 1875, and between the chamber music works just mentioned, Dvořák achieved two other compositions which are of importance. One of these is the first cycle of Moravian Duets (op.20) which he wrote in March of that year. They were written at the instigation of his friends Jan and Marie Neff and, according to the printed Simrock Edition, were dedicated to Marie Neff. It

appears that one day Neff had shown Dvořák a collection of
Moravian songs and had suggested that he should provide a
setting for these melodies. However, Dvořák preferred to
write his own tunes and only use the texts. Both the Neffs were
delighted with the result and urged him to compose others.
Three more cycles were to follow in 1876/77, but it should be
noted that, whereas the first cycle of four Duets was written for
Soprano, *Tenor* and Piano, the subsequent three cycles were
set for Soprano, *Alto* and Piano. Also, in 1880, Dvořák
selected five songs from the second and third cycles and re-
arranged them for four women's voices *a cappella*.

Enough has already been said about the great impression
which these Duets made on Brahms and then on Simrock,
about the way in which they opened the German publishing
field for him, and the enthusiasm with which they were
received abroad – albeit under the German title *Klänge aus
Mähren*, which was far from Dvořák's intention. Nowadays,
despite their charm and their melodiousness, we hear them
but rarely, except on the radio or on gramophone records.
They share the fate of so much of Dvořák's – and not only
Dvořák's – music for this sort of combination. This also applies
to many of his works for piano solo and piano duet. For this
music was in vogue in an age which knew nothing of
mechanical reproduction media, an age in which there was still
vital music-making in the home, when the *salon* still flourished.
It is sad that much beautiful music should have become so
neglected, but in view of our so-called 'civilization' and our
'progress', it is also inevitable.

The other work from the first half of 1875, in a sense, stands
in direct contrast to the foregoing. This is the Serenade in E for
string orchestra (op.22) composed between 3 and 14 May. It is
perhaps the earliest of Dvořák's works which is generally
known to concert audiences of our time, and it has retained its
popularity ever since its first performance on 10 December
1876, when Adolf Čech conducted it in Prague. Its five
movements have an irresistible charm, particularly the way in
which the opening melody returns towards the end of the

Finale – and I have often wondered whether Elgar may have been influenced in this respect when *he* came to write *his* Serenade for Strings. On a much more prosaic plane it can also be argued that Dvořák's Serenade owes its popularity to a certain extent to the fact that, for any string orchestra, the repertoire of 19th century music is exceedingly limited.

Towards the middle of 1875 Dvořák embarked on his next symphony, the one in F, and completed it in one fell swoop between 15 June and 23 July. In order of composition it was No. 5, and he gave it the opus number 24 – Simrock eventually published it in 1888 as No. 3, op.76, after Dvořák had made some minor revisions in 1887. We have seen how the G major String Quintet divides Dvořák's fourteen string quartets into two halves, and in a somewhat similar manner the F major Symphony No. 5, numerically and otherwise as well, forms the central pillar of Dvořák's nine compositions in this field. No. 5 is a homogeneous whole, conceived with singularity of vision and, although surpassed in certain respects by its successors, it is the first of his symphonies which is often included in concert programmes – and not just as a museum piece which requires an apologia in the programme notes. It is dictated by Dvořák's Bohemian nature throughout, without any Wagnerian intrusions, and it has often been described as his 'pastoral' symphony, although in the last movement thunder clouds appear on the horizon. We can gauge the symphonic mastery which Dvořák had now reached by just listening to the transition from the second to the third movement. The Finale is outstanding in its economy of means, which make it one of the finest symphonic movements Dvořák had composed up to that time. His predeliction for exploiting key relationships through a wide range is particularly pronounced, and in the way in which he handled these matters one is somehow reminded of Schubert's approach to tonality and modulation. It is also worth noting that the opening motto of the first movement recurs at the very end of the Finale. Dvořák wrote the work in 1875 – we find the same feature only in Bruckner in 1874 (Symphony No. 3); Brahms used it in 1884 (Symphony

No. 3) and César Franck in 1888 (Symphony in D minor).
Shortly before publication, Dvořák asked the conductor Hans
von Bülow whether he would accept the dedication. Von
Bülow replied in his most warm-hearted vein saying:

> 'A dedication from you – next to Brahms the most
> divinely gifted composer of the present time – is a higher
> decoration than any sort of Grand Cross from the hands
> of a Prince.' (See illustration 42).

The symphony had its first performance in Prague under the
baton of Adolf Čech in March 1879, and it was the first time
since Smetana had played the Symphony No. 3 five years
earlier that a complete Dvořák symphony was heard there in
public. Dvořák himself conducted the Symphony in F in Brno
ten months later, but after that it fell into complete neglect until
August Manns performed it in the London Crystal Palace in
April 1888.

The rest of 1875, from July or August until December,
Dvořák concentrated entirely on the compostion of his opera
Vanda which has already been discussed. But during that
period tragedy struck the Dvořák household for the first time:
on 19 September 1875 their second child, a daughter Josefa,
was born, only to die two days later. This must have been a
great blow to Dvořák, who adored children, but we know little
of his feelings, for he rarely spoke – let alone wrote – about
personal matters. However, the two chamber music works
which he composed in January 1876 speak their own language,
for both the Piano Trio in G minor (op.26) as well as the String
Quartet in E major (originally op.27, but published by Simrock
as op.80) seem to reflect his mood to a certain extent. In a G
minor work this is not particularly surprising, and it must be
admitted that this Piano Trio is not one of Dvořák's best
works. The Finale in particular is weak, although he makes
much of the interplay of the minor and the major – a peculiar
characteristic of Bohemian music typical of Dvořák. By
contrast, the String Quartet No. 8 in E major marks the
beginning of those seven string quartets which show Dvořák in

his maturity. It is strange that, although it is written in a so-called 'bright' key, a certain sadness makes itself felt throughout. This sadness is particularly apparent in the second movement, *Andante con moto*, which really fore-shadows the *Dumka* so frequent in his later works, although in this instance he did not yet entitle the movement as such.

If one looks through Dvořák's compositions in chronological order, there is one general trend which stands out unmis-takably: whenever he had written one or more major works, he turned his mind to small-scale compositions, almost as though he felt in need of relaxation. 1875 had brought forth three important chamber music works, the Serenade for Strings, the Symphony in F and the opera *Vanda*, and during the first month of 1876 another two chamber music works had come into being. Now, from February until July, he turned to lighter fare: a couple of Minuets for piano and various groups of songs, amongst them the second and third cycles of Moravian Duets. The only major work with which he toyed was a *Stabat Mater* for which he made some sketches, but these he then put aside. Nor was there much excitement on the personal front: both the String Quintet in G and *Vanda* had their first performances in Prague, but apart from that his life must have been taken up with his organist's duties at St. Adalbert and his teaching. The only other notable event in that year 1876 was the birth of a daughter Růžena on 18 September, just one year after the short-lived Josefa, so now there were two children in the house.

In August Dvořák turned to something meatier again and set to work on his one and only Piano Concerto (op.33) in G minor, which he completed by 14 September. Forgetting the incomplete Cello Concerto of 1865, it is the first of three full-length concertos for solo instrument and orchestra which Dvořák was to compose. Of the three, the Piano Concerto is the one which is most seldom heard, and there can be no denying that it does not make the same impact as the later concertos for violin and for cello. It is true that fundamentally Dvořák was a string player, and already in the earlier Piano

Trios and the Piano Quartet there is some awkwardness in his attempt to integrate the piano with other instruments, but although Dvořák was by no means a virtuoso pianist, he played the piano well. The argument that in the Piano Concerto he kept the piano part relatively simple because of his own technical limitations will not hold water because, after all, he wrote it for the Czech virtuoso Karel ze Slavkovských. It is my firm belief that Dvořák wrote the solo part the way he did so that it should fuse into a symphonic whole with the modest orchestral forces which he employed. The result is a work of noble simplicity. Lack of the virtuoso element has impeded the progress of the concerto, and it only became more widely known after the noted professor for piano Vilém Kurz revised the solo part to make it more brilliant. It was in this revised version that it was customarily performed until recently. Now some pianists revert to the original, and it can only be hoped that eventually others will not consider it too trifling or beneath their dignity. We must remember that, not all that many decades ago, they viewed the piano concertos of Wolfgang Amadeus Mozart in the same light.

Two other compositions from that year 1876 remain to be mentioned, both for piano and both written in December: a *Dumka* and a *Tema con variazioni*. The *Tema con variazioni* (op.36) is important only in as much as it is one of the few longish compositions for piano which Dvořák wrote, most of them being short pieces and dances, though at times these are grouped together. But more important is the *Dumka* (op.35), for this is the first time that Dvořák gave the official title *Dumka* to a piece of music. Later he was to make use of it frequently, and the term has probably become best known through the Piano Trio of 1890/91 which is known world-wide as the *Dumky* Trio. The word *Dumka* is of Ukrainian origin and virtually untranslatable; it has been variously rendered as 'Elegy', 'Plaint', 'Lament' – perhaps the German word *Weltschmerz* comes nearest to it, although some of Dvořák's *Dumkas* can be quite lively affairs too.

1877 was a year which brought many ups and downs in Dvořák's life. In the early months he was again awarded the Austrian State Grant which had now been increased to 500 Gulden, and it was perhaps due to this that he could afford to resign from his post at St. Adalbert in February. He had been organist there for precisely three years, and it should be noted that, apart from the academic appointments which he later held at the Conservatoria of Prague and New York, this was the last salaried position which he occupied. Then, in July, he went on a walking tour in central and southern Bohemia with his young friend and colleague, Leoš Janáček, who was then 23 years old and who, a few weeks earlier, had conducted a performance of Dvořák's Serenade for Strings in Brno. At the end of that holiday – probably the first proper holiday Dvořák had ever had – he spent some days with his friend Alois Göbl at Sychrov.

A few words must be said about Göbl, for far too little is mentioned about him in the general literature on Dvořák. Göbl was a very talented singer, and Dvořák first made his acquaintance when he was a viola player at the National Theatre. The acquaintance soon developed into a friendship, and Göbl remained a close friend for the rest of Dvořák's life. However, when Göbl realized that he would never 'make the grade' as a truly great singer, he took on a position as teacher on the estate of Prince Rohan in Sychrov near Turnov in Bohemia and eventually became Secretary to the Prince. We owe Göbl a great debt of gratitude. It has been mentioned more than once that Dvořák was of a taciturn nature and was disinclined to speak or write about his feelings. A little story from the 'Musical Memoirs' by Ladislav Dolanský may serve as an example of this:

> 'Once on a Sunday forenoon we met at Velebin Urbánek's shop. Dvořák invited me to go to a wine-shop. I was not accustomed at that time to drink anything in the forenoon and was not very willing to comply. But Dvořák insisted: "Please do me the favour, I should not go alone."

So I said I would and we sat down in Masaryk's little Moravian wine-shop. I began a conversation several times but Dvořák did not reply. I recalled his recent visit to Písek. And still Dvořák remained silent. So I fell silent, too, and we sat opposite each other without a word. When Dvořák had finished his glass, we paid and went out. In the street he shook me warmly by the hand and said: "You don't know how grateful I am that you went with me; you have done me a great service," and we parted . . .'

With Göbl, somehow, he was much more open. He wrote about his works, he wrote about his personal feelings, and it is through the correspondence which he regularly entertained with Göbl that we gain so much valuable insight into the inner man who was Dvořák.

After this summer holiday, disaster struck again in the home of Dvořák. On 13 August 1877, their daughter Růžena died, barely eleven months old, and she was followed less than four weeks later by her older brother Otakar (I) who died of smallpox on 8 September, Dvořák's 36th birthday. So Anna and Antonín found themselves childless, but they were to be recompensed: nine months almost to the day after the death of Otakar, their daughter Otilie (Otilka) was born on 6 June 1878. She was the first of the six children who were to survive their father, and she is perhaps best known for the fact that later she married Dvořák's pupil, the composer Josef Suk.

Another major change was Dvořák's move to a new home. Probably the quarters in Na Rybníčku 14 had become too cramped, the surrounding noise of instruments being practised was becoming intolerable, and improved financial conditions made the change possible. So in November 1877 Dvořák moved to a flat in the Žitná 10. The house is nowadays No. 14, and it should perhaps be mentioned that in those days, when Prague was largely German-speaking, the street was known as the *Korngasse*, the form in which it usually appears in Dvořák's correspondence. This house remained Dvořák's home until his dying day, although in May 1880 he exchanged the flat at the rear of the house for one facing the street. But it is in the Žitná No. 10 – no matter in which flat – that he received visitors such as Brahms and Simrock, Grieg and Tchaikovsky, and many other famous musicians. The last event of that year 1877 was the abortive trip to Vienna in December, when he failed to meet Brahms but made the acquaintance of Hanslick.

Musically 1877 is marked by a number of important compositions. Strangely enough, the first of them is by no means 'major', but has a special bearing on matters: in January he composed three songs for male chorus which would not deserve particular mention if it were not for the fact that the third of them, *Já jsem huslař* ('I am a fiddler'), was later that year to become the main theme of his Symphonic Variations. Dvořák returned to his obsession with opera and started composing 'The Cunning Peasant', which he completed after his holiday with Janáček. In the meantime he also found time to write an *Ave Maria*, and the fourth and last major cycle of Moravian Duets. These he followed up with the Symphonic Variations (op.78) already mentioned, on a theme developed from 'I am a fiddler'. Dvořák started on them on 6 August and completed the composition on 28 September 1877. During this period and while he was working on these, his daughter Růžena and his son Otakar (I) died. Many writers claim that there is an underlying feeling of rebellion against fate in the music, but I have always failed to detect anything of the sort. However, these Variations mark the turning point towards Dvořák's customarily termed 'nationalistic period'. From here onwards, and for quite a few years to come, Dvořák is uninhibitedly, unashamedly and outspokenly Bohemian and free from outside influences. The title which he gave to the work may also cause some raised eyebrows: 'Symphonic Variations on an original theme from the part-song "I am a fiddler" for full orchestra, composed and muddled up by Antonín Dvořák'.* So, despite beard and stern outward

*Sinfonické variace na původné thema ze sboru 'Já som guslar' pro velký orkestr složil a zmotal Antonín Dvořák.

appearance, the Great Man had a sense of humour as well!

The Variations had their first performance on 2 December 1877 in a concert on Žofín Island (an islet in the river Vltava, within Prague) under the direction of Ludevít Procházka, and the public acclaimed it wildly, but it was a charity concert and the press took no notice of it. Dvořák was deeply hurt, relegated the score to one of the bottom drawers of his writing desk, and it did not see the light of day again until he offered it to Hans Richter in 1887 for performance in London. Richter was enthusiastic, and in a letter from London wrote to Dvořák on 13 May 1887:

> 'I come positively carried away by the first rehearsal for the Third Concert at which we are playing your "Symphonic Variations". It is a magnificent work! I am glad to be the first to perform it in London, but why have you kept it back so long? These Variations can take their place among the best of your compositions. I shall send you news of the performance.
> P.S. They will be on the programme of the next Philharmonic Concerts in Vienna.'

From then onwards the Symphonic Variations made their way throughout the world, they became one of Dvořák's best-loved works, and even Simrock – who did not like 'long' and 'serious' compositions – deigned to publish them in 1888, although under the completely fictitious opus number 78 (it should have been op.28).

If, in my view, there is no feeling of depression or sadness over the death of his two children in the Symphonic Variations, matters are very different in Dvořák's next major work. He took out the sketches for the *Stabat Mater* made in the first half of 1876, and scored the complete work in the months of October/November 1877. Apart from a lost Mass in B flat of his student days, this was Dvořák's first large-scale liturgical work and reflects the grief which he must have felt at that time. The *Stabat Mater* has been described as 'the first Oratorio of modern Czech music'. Not only did it bring him world-wide fame, it was also the work which truly opened the door to England for him.

Taken as a whole, the *Stabat Mater* leaves two immediate impressions: one is that of a deep and heart-felt religious belief, the other is that of natural and Bohemian melodiousness. The two merge into an entity. It is at one and the same time a moving and an enjoyable work. It must be admitted that some movements are weaker than others, in particular the somewhat trite *Fac me vere*, but even so I would still prefer any day to listen to this work than to the more popular *Stabat Mater* by Rossini with its operatic overtones. What is perhaps most striking – and this may sound paradoxical – is that in this sacred oratorio the innate symphonist and instrumental composer in Dvořák comes to the fore so strongly. Not only does he write an orchestral introduction of close on five minutes' duration before we first hear the words *Stabat Mater* softly muttered by the voices, but this orchestral introduction could almost be described as a miniature symphonic summing-up of Jacopone da Todi's immortal poem: the expression of hope in divine salvation contrasted with the human anguish of the mother. Nor does this promising opening disappoint us except in isolated moments. It is the music, the sound of the orchestra, which propagates the message rather than the text.

There seems to be no rational explanation why this great choral work had to wait for just over three years for its first performance, and even then the choice of date for that first performance seems now to have been both strange and singularly inappropriate: it took place in Prague on 23 December 1880, the day before Christmas Eve, and again that staunch supporter of Dvořák's music, Adolf Čech, conducted. In 1881 Simrock published it, and within the next few years the *Stabat Mater* became a 'draw' all over Europe and America.

Shortly after completing the *Stabat Mater* Dvořák received the good news from Vienna that he had once more been awarded the Austrian State Grant which had now been increased to 600 Gulden. Possibly it was this which stimulated him to make the trip to Vienna in December where, as we know, he missed Brahms but met Hanslick, and possibly it was also with all these things combined in his mind that he was inspired to write his last major work in that eventful year 1877: his String Quartet No. 9 in D minor (op.34). The mood of this quartet is subdued, despite the second movement which is marked *Allegretto scherzando* and headed *Alla polka*. This is not to say that it is in any way doleful. Opinions are divided as to whether Dvořák was already thinking in terms of a dedication to Brahms at the time of the composition, or whether this dedication only came about after the two men had entered into correspondence. I tend to the former assumption, because Dvořák wrote his letter to Brahms on 3 December 1877 and began work on the quartet only four days later. But more important, this D minor Quartet shares a certain classical severity with only one other Dvořák String Quartet, namely No. 11 in C major (op.61) of 1881, which he wrote at the request of – and dedicated to – the violinist and *Hofkapellmeister* Josef Hellmesberger. In both cases, I think, he felt a particular responsibility because the dedicatees were great Viennese musicians, and Vienna was considered by the whole world – and particularly by the Viennese themselves – to be the place with a proprietory right to the genus String Quartet. What a daunting task to write for Them! Nevertheless, Dvořák completed the work in less than a fortnight, so it is not surprising that he 'wrote somewhat hurriedly' which caused Brahms to rebuke him gently in his letter of March 1878. To my mind it is, despite this, a finer quartet than certain more popular ones from Dvořák's pen.

The years that followed, 1878-80, saw hardly any basic change in Dvořák's personal life. For him and his wife the most important events must have been the births of their two daughters Otilie (6 June 1878) and Anna (13 January 1880). Having lost their first three children so tragically, these two girls meant the start of a new family. No doubt also the move to the more pleasant flat on the street side of the Žitná No. 10 in

May 1880 must have added greatly to the comfort of their lives. But in the main, and leaving out various minor excursions and holidays which will be mentioned, these years were marked by a steady growth in musical stature, the first honours conferred on Dvořák, increased travel on 'musical business', an equally steady increase in performances and publications, but above all a tremendous flow of compositions.

The first work of that period came into being in January 1878: a second serenade, the so-called Serenade for Wind Instruments in D minor (op.44) – 'so-called' because the orchestration also comprises cello and double bass. In one sense, as the work begins with a March which makes another appearance towards the end of the Finale, Dvořák seems to be turning back to the form of the serenade as conceived by Haydn and Mozart, but on the other hand he freely allows Bohemian elements, rhythms and melodies to pervade the work as a whole. It is particularly noticeable that every one of its four movements begins with a rising fourth; whether this is accident or design on Dvořák's part is difficult to tell. Nevertheless, these fourths provide a unifying factor. The autograph bears no dedication, but when Simrock came to print the Serenade in 1879, Dvořák dedicated it to Louis Ehlert.

Ehlert was one of Germany's leading music critics of the time. His publications appeared mainly in Berlin, although he himself lived in Wiesbaden. Shortly after they were published he got to know the Moravian Duets and the first set of Slavonic Dances (in their piano duet version), and on 15 November 1878 a review of his appeared in the Berlin *Nationalzeitung*. A more glowing write-up can hardly be imagined:

'. . . Here at last is a hundred per cent talent and, what is more, a completely natural talent. I consider the Slavonic Dances to be a work which will make its triumphant way through the world in the same way as Brahms' Hungarian Dances. . . . Divine Providence flows through this music and that is why it is altogether popular. Not a trace of arti-ficiality or constraint . . . here we are confronted with

perfected works of art and not perhaps with some pastiche
stuck together from scraps of national melody. . . .'

On the strength of this article – which had the effect of causing
a veritable run on the Duets and Dances in all music-shops of
Germany – Dvořák and Ehlert began to correspond with each
other and soon also became acquainted personally. Ehlert
actively continued his support of Dvořák throughout the
ensuing years, and the friendship between the two men only
came to an end with Ehlert's death in January 1884, just before
Dvořák set off on his first journey to England.

Shortly after the Serenade was completed, the 'Cunning
Peasant' had its first performance at the National Theatre in
Prague in January, and it may perhaps be due to the initial
success of this opera that Dvořák was stimulated to examine a
libretto by Zeyer, *Šarká*, but he never pursued the matter any
further. Instead, he embarked on a project which he had
cherished ever since writing that Rhapsody in A minor (op.14)
in 1874 which he later renamed 'Symphonic Poem': that of
composing a number of Slavonic Rhapsodies. The first of
these, in D major, he wrote in February/March 1878, but
before he could start on the next one, there came the
commission from Simrock to compose the Slavonic Dances,
and he set to work on them immediately. The chronology of his
compostions now becomes somewhat confused, as Dvořák
followed a course which was unusual for him in that works
overlap a good deal. He completed the Slavonic Rhapsody
No. 1 on 17 March 1878, and the following day began with the
composition of the first set of Slavonic Dances in their piano
duet version. As a whole, that version was not completed until
7 May, but in between he had already begun with the
orchestration of three of the Dances. Also, while in the final
stages of composing the piano duet version, he tossed off five
Bagatelles (*Maličkosti*) for two violins, cello and harmonium –
a charming little group of pieces ideally suited for amateur
music-making in the home. They are completely neglected,
which is not surprising: when do you have a harmonium in a
chamber music recital? But on musical grounds this neglect

cannot be justifed, for in these unpretentious pieces Dvořák shows his true nature: they are melodious, easy to listen to, and they represent all that was nearest and dearest to Dvořák's heart – a homely atmosphere, family, friends, warmth.

Then, before settling down in earnest to the orchestration of the Slavonic Dances, he wrote, in May 1878, what is indubitably one of his greatest chamber music works: his one and only String Sextet. In addition to this he composed the first of two *Furiants* for piano, and while working on the orchestration of the Dances he managed to fit in some minor vocal works as well. It is of interest to note that during this period the private first performance of Smetana's Quartet 'From my Life' took place at the home of Dvořák's friend J. Srb-Debrnov (to whom the Bagatelles are dedicated) with Dvořák himself playing the viola part. Despite the obvious pressure of work he snatched a brief holiday in the Bohemian Forest as well as a visit to his friend Göbl in Sychrov.

That the first set of Slavonic Dances was a roaring success at home and abroad has been mentioned more than once, and they continue to be firm favourites in our present-day music-life. The first set (op.46) always seems to have enjoyed greater popularity than the second (op.72) of 1886/87. With the exception of No. 2, which is of Serbian origin, the first set is based entirely on Bohemian rhythms – *Furiant, Sousedská, Polka, Skočná* – while the second set consists of dances from a variety of Slavonic countries. It should also be noted that, although obviously Dvořák must have been influenced by many popular folk-dances which he had come to know well both in childhood and while playing in the Komzák band, he never used any original folk-melodies in those Dances, but always invented his own tunes in the true Bohemian spirit.

The moment the Slavonic Dances were finished – and, presumably, sent off to Simrock post-haste – Dvořák went back to his Slavonic Rhapsodies and completed No. 2 (in G minor) and No. 3 (in A flat major) between 20 August and 3 December 1878. It is worth noting that Simrock was so encouraged by the success of the Moravian Duets and the Slavonic Dances that, on the strength of it, he bought all three Slavonic Rhapsodies (published together as op.45), the Bagatelles and the D minor Serenade in a batch, paid Dvořák 1700 Marks for them and issued them all in 1879/80. The first two Rhapsodies had their first performance in Prague on 17 November 1878 when the Wind Serenade also had its première, with Dvořák himself conducting, and it must have been a most memorable day for him, as it was the first concert ever consisting solely of his works. A matter of ten days later he was elected a Committee Member of the Society of Artists (*Umělecká beseda*) so that, when later in November he travelled to Berlin to have his first personal meeting with Simrock, he must have felt infinitely surer of himself than had been the case a few months earlier.

On his return to Prague he completed the third of the Slavonic Rhapsodies and a few days later he was off to Vienna where, at long last, he met his idol Brahms. One little amusing item in connection with this trip bears mention: Dvořák was a locomotive enthusiast – about which more later – and during his journey to Vienna he must have been exceedingly busy 'locomotive-spotting'. Yet, despite his great hobby, he also managed to write five part-songs while on the train! On the way back he went via Brno (Brünn) to be present at a concert on 15 December 1878 in which Leoš Janáček conducted the first performance of a group of three Slavonic Folk-Songs by Dvořák for male chorus and piano, with the composer himself at the piano. This is not so important, but in the same programme Janáček also conducted the first performance of his own early Suite for Strings *Idyla*, and I have often wondered whether memories of that performance and particularly the fifth movement of the Suite may not have lingered in Dvořák's subconscious mind when, years later, he composed his Cello Concerto . . .

For the Christmas celebrations he was, as usual, back with

his family, but this did not stop him from starting a new string quartet exceptionally on Christmas Day – No. 10 in E flat (op.51). Again it has a *Dumka* as its second movement, but this time it is a *Dumka* interrupted by fast sections reminiscent of a *Furiant* and therefore does not form the slow movement proper: that is reserved for the third movement, *Romanza*. Considering the speed with which Dvořák composed at that time, it may seem surprising that he did not complete the quartet until 28 March 1879, but then there were important interventions. Early in 1879 both Brahms and Simrock visited him in Prague, there were some first performances (including that of Symphony No. 5), and various commissioned compositions to attend to, such as the Festival March (*Slavnostní pochod*, op.54) in honour of the Silver Wedding of Franz Josef and Elisabeth of Austria, as well as the 149th Psalm for the Hlahol Choral Society. This Psalm was first heard in Prague in March 1879 under Karel Knittl. In February of that year, without being commissioned, Dvořák also wrote the delightful little *Mazurek* for violin and piano (op.49) which he immediately orchestrated, dedicating it to Sarasate. Also it is worth mentioning that August Manns gave the first English performance of three of the Slavonic Dances in the Crystal Palace in London on 15 February 1879 – as far as I can ascertain the first public performance of a major Dvořák work in England.

March and April 1879 were months of travel. He went to Berlin (presumably to see Simrock) and to Leipzig to pay a call on Röder, the famous engraver. On his return to Prague he embarked on his next orchestral work, a Suite for Orchestra in D which has since become known as the 'Czech Suite' (op.39). In this work Dvořák seems to have found his inspiration flowing more readily than when writing the D minor Serenade fifteen months earlier. But a new problem arose: Dvořák had given a verbal undertaking to Simrock during his Berlin visit that he should have first option on all new compositions. Schlesinger on the other hand offered more favourable terms for the Czech Suite, and so it went to him under a fictitiously early opus number. Like Beethoven, Dvořák had a strong practical bent when dealing with his publishers!

In June 1879 the Dvořák family went to Sychrov for their summer holidays, and from there Antonín visited Berlin for the second time that year in July for what must surely have been a major event for him. The famous violinist Joseph Joachim, once again through the efforts of Johannes Brahms, had been alerted to that up-and-coming, talented composer Antonín Dvořák, and on 29 July 1879 Joachim gave a private soirée in Dvořák's honour at his Berlin home. There, in the composer's presence, both the Sextet and the E flat String Quartet had their first hearing. From all accounts Dvořák was shy and overawed at being surrounded by so many notables of the German musical world, but both the Sextet and the Quartet were an eminent success. It must have been the first time since the days of the many Bohemian *émigrés* mentioned in the introductory chapter that Czech chamber music works had their first performance outside the borders of their composers' native country. Both Joachim and Hellmesberger took to the Sextet and played it wherever and whenever they could. This is not surprising, for its combination of classical form and Bohemian exuberance make this work come as near to perfection as one can hope for on this earth. The way in which a *Dumka* and a *Furiant* are integrated into the whole is sheer genius, even though the *Furiant* movement is not a *Furiant* proper, lacking its characteristic cross-rhythm. No wonder that Alec Robertson refers to it as 'that excellent travel poster'!

As for the Quartet in E flat Dvořák found an equally enthusiastic protagonist in Jean Becker, the first violin of the Florentine Quartet to whom the work is dedicated. This Quartet performed the work wherever they went. Unfortunately Simrock had not managed to publish the parts in time for Becker to include it in the programmes of their Swiss tour of 1879, and so the first performance was given in Prague by Sobotka and his Quartet in December, but thereafter the Florentine Quartet had it in their standard repertoire.

We now come to Dvořák's second full-length concerto, the

one for Violin and Orchestra in A minor (op.53). Simrock had
suggested a Violin Concerto to him, and he began sketching it
in July 1879 before going to Berlin where he was to meet
Joachim, though we cannot be certain whether he had this
visit in mind at the time. But this is immaterial, for the fact
remains that throughout the composition of this work Joachim
was Dvořák's mentor and helpmate.

From Berlin Dvořák returned to his family at Sychrov and
then travelled about a good deal in Bohemia and Austria until
he finally settled in at home in Prague again at the beginning of
September. But during that period he was by no means idle:
the first version of the Violin Concerto was completed in the
first half of September 1879, and in between he had still found
time to compose some vocal works as well as an overture for
Vanda. Unfortunately we know relatively little of the first
version of the concerto as Dvořák used many of its pages
when writing the second version, at the same time destroying
the majority of those pages for which he had no further use.
This second and final version – final version, that is, if we ignore
some minor revisions of 1882 – he composed in April/May
1880 after detailed consultations with Joachim, to whom the
work is dedicated. However, in the end it was not Joachim but
František Ondříček who gave the first performance in Prague
in October 1883, and apparently Joachim never played it in
public. Although the concerto does not measure up to those
of Beethoven and Brahms – what other violin concerto does? –
it is a work of great beauty, in my opinion superior to that much
more popular Violin Concerto by Max Bruch, and it is
incomprehensible that though several violinists outside
Czechoslovakia have taken it into their repertoire, performances are still relatively infrequent. It goes without saying that
the Finale, which is in Rondo form, is for the most part based
on a *Furiant* rhythm, with a *Dumka* as an interlude.

Much of what has been said about the Piano Concerto also
applies to the Violin Concerto and to the considerably later
Cello Concerto. Both works, though they are true concertos,
are symphonic in concept. However, in both cases, the soloist

has much more scope for displaying his virtuosity than in the Piano Concerto. Partly this may be because Dvořák had matured even more, particularly through his constant contact with Brahms and his music; partly because, being a string player himself, he may have found the violin and the cello more congenial. It should be noted most emphatically that, following the examples of Beethoven in the Piano Concerto in E flat, of Schumann, Brahms (except for his Violin Concerto, also written for Joachim) and Tchaikovsky, he did not allow his soloist any liberties as regards cadenzas: if he wanted a cadenza, he wrote it himself.

During the months between composing the two versions of the Violin Concerto Dvořák spent some time revising other scores, particularly the *Hymnus*. As far as new works are concerned he concentrated on smaller forms, mainly compositions for the piano: the twelve Silhouettes (op.8), a Polonaise, as well as the eight Waltzes (op.54) among others. Nor must we forget the lovely Gypsy Songs (op.55) which he wrote early in 1880, if only because the fourth of these, 'Songs my Mother taught me', eventually became what is probably the best known of all of Dvořák's songs. As for the Silhouettes, two points are of interest. The first is that in No. 6 there is a turn of phrase which seems to foreshadow the first of Brahms' *Intermezzi* op.117 of 1892. The other is that once again he gave the Silhouettes a very low opus number in order to be able to sell them to Hofmeister – although in this instance he may have placated his conscience to a certain extent by the knowledge that some of the sketches went back to 1870 or 1872.

Nor were these last months of 1879 and the early part of 1880 uneventful in other respects. In September 1879 the third of the three Slavonic Rhapsodies had its first performance under Taubert in Berlin, and only six weeks later the Joachim Quartet with two extra players gave the *public* première of the Sextet, also in Berlin. But from the point of view of professional advancement, most important was Dvořák's election as Chairman of the Music Section of the Society of Artists in Prague on 12 November 1879. In a sense this put a final,

definitive stamp on Dvořák, now aged 38, as a composer of
note. Two days after receiving this honour Dvořák travelled to
Vienna to be present at the first Viennese performance of his
Slavonic Rhapsody No.3 which Hans Richter conducted. It
was during this visit that he met Richter personally and that
Richter asked him to write a symphony for the Vienna
Philharmonic Society. The importance of Richter's friendship
for Dvořák and the high esteem in which he held Dvořák's
music cannot be stressed too strongly. Richter had become a
well-known figure on the English musical scene ever since he
had shared the conductorship of the famous Wagner concerts
in the London Albert Hall in 1877 with Wagner himself. From
1879 onwards he conducted an annual series of orchestral
concerts in London which became known as the Richter
Concerts, and his strong involvement with English musical life
continued up to 1911, when he resigned from the conductorship of the Hallé Orchestra in Manchester. It is thanks to the
fervour with which Richter propagated Dvořák's music that
England became Dvořák's firmest stronghold outside his
homeland, for let it not be forgotten that, in central Europe,
Dvořák was mainly known for his Moravian Duets, his
Slavonic Dances and other compositions on a smaller scale. It
was Richter (and later Hans von Bülow) who were the
champions of his large symphonic and choral works and
endeared them to the English and also to the Viennese.

1880 started auspiciously. In the very first days of January
Dvořák went to Brno to conduct his Symphony No. 5 and the
Slavonic Rhapsody No. 2, and after his return to Prague his
daughter Anna was born on 13 January. As a whole it was a
good year, especially for performances abroad: Dresden
heard the D minor Serenade, Leipzig the Slavonic Dances,
Joachim programmed the Sextet in London, Hamburg put on
the first ever all-Dvořák concert outside the Czech Lands, and
England also was presented with the Slavonic Rhapsodies
No. 3 (London, under Richter) and No. 1 (Manchester, under

Hallé) as well as the E flat String Quartet – so there was no question any more of Dvořák being 'a local product for a local market'. But, generally speaking, it was the Rhapsody No. 3 which caught on particularly, and the list of performances of that work which took place during the 1879/80 concert season in places as far apart as Budapest and Cincinnati is indeed imposing.

His personal life was fairly uneventful. In February, Brahms and Joachim came to Prague for a joint concert, and of course they visited Dvořák at his home. It may have been this visit which in March stimulated Dvořák to abandon small-scale compositions for something more ambitious: the Violin Sonata in F major (op.57). The work bears no dedication, except for the famous *Zaplať pań Bůh*, but there can be no doubt that it was intended as a tribute to Joseph Joachim. Apart from the Sonatina in G major (op.100) which he wrote in New York it is the only work in this form from Dvořák's pen, and again it had its first performance in a private circle in Joachim's house when Dvořák visited Berlin at the end of March 1880 in order to discuss the Violin concerto with him. As has been said, the second version of the Concerto occupied most of Dvořák's time during the ensuing months (as probably did the move to the flat on the street side in the Žitná No. 10); he was also busy writing a number of short pieces for piano, which would have pleased Simrock greatly – but they went to other publishers.

At that time Dvořák went through a difficult phase. He knew that with all these short pieces of *salon*-music and works for amateur musicians he could win the favour of his publishers, his public, and also earn good fees. It would have been very easy for him to continue in this vein, but it seems that he had a change of mind. We do not know the precise reasons: in July 1880 he went to Vysoká for the first time for a break – Vysoká being the country estate of Count Kaunic, the husband of his former great love and now his sister-in-law Josefina Čermáková – and in those rustic surroundings he may have had the chance of meditating and coming to terms with himself. Next he went to Wiesbaden to visit Louis Ehlert, and those meetings may have been another contributing factor. Lastly, he may have remembered that, when meeting Hans Richter in Vienna in November 1879 on the occasion of the Viennese première of the Slavonic Rhapsody No. 3, he had promised Richter a symphony. Whether it was a result of one or several of these considerations is of little importance. It suffices that, on 27 August 1880, he settled down to his next Symphony, No. 6 in D major, and allowed nothing to interrupt his work until it was completed on 15 October 1880, with the exception of two short trips to Chrudim (for the first performance of his Violin Sonata) and to Zlonice to take part in a charity concert in order to raise funds for a memorial to his former teacher Antonín Liehmann.

Five years had passed since he had completed his Symphony No. 5 in F, so it is not surprising that the new symphony represents a great advance on all that had gone before in this field. Dvořák devoted all his energies to this Symphony No. 6, and the result justified the effort. This Symphony in D is the first of what are commonly described as 'the last great four symphonies'. Every authority seems to pick a different one of these four as being *the* greatest, which is nonsense. Each of them has a character uniquely its own, every one of them is great, masterly and beautiful, and comparisons get us nowhere, nor does the statement that the D major Symphony should be compared to Brahms' Symphony No. 2 in the same key. For myself, the Sixth is my favourite. The first movement, with its horn calls, irresistibly conjures up a vision of the Bohemian Forest, the slow movement is infused with a Schubertian lyricism, and the third movement, *Scherzo (Furiant)*, is a *Furiant* cast into true symphonic form, worthy of comparison with the great *Furiant* in Smetana's 'Bartered Bride'. But what is all-important is that in *this* Symphony Dvořák at last solves the problem of the Finale. It proceeds with complete confidence. Dvořák does not allow himself to be sidetracked. It is in fact the most convincing Finale he ever composed. Although Dvořák dedicated his Symphony No. 6 to Hans Richter, it was again

Adolf Čech who conducted the première in Prague on 25 March 1881. Richter conducted it in London in May 1882, but he was beaten to the first English performance by the indefatigable August Manns who had anticipated him by a matter of three weeks. Incidentally, Richter also missed out on the Viennese première which was conducted by Gericke in February 1883.* Simrock, probably impressed by Richter's advocacy of the work, not surprisingly snapped it up – and published it in 1882 as No. 1! It proved to be a resounding success in many countries of Europe as well as in America.

As usual, having achieved a major work, Dvořák turned to miniatures. None of these are of great importance except that, at the request of Simrock, he orchestrated five of Brahms' Hungarian Dances. It was only at the very end of 1880 – on 30 December, to be precise – that he embarked on another work, which, though consisting of ten basically unrelated pieces for piano duet, is usually played as a ten-movement work: the Legends (op.59). The piano duet version was completed by March 1881, and in November and December of that year he orchestrated it, dedicating it to Hanslick. Simrock published both versions in 1881 and 1882 respectively. It is quite likely that, while composing the Legends, Dvořák had the popularity of the Slavonic Dances in mind but, if this was the case, both he and Simrock must have been disappointed, for the Legends never caught on in the same way. One reason may be that, melodious and beautiful as they are, they are really more suited to the medium of the piano duet, whereas the Slavonic Dances come off best in their orchestral garb.

In the first days of January 1881 Dvořák began to study the libretto of *Dimitrij*, for once again he felt an inner urge to turn

---

*Richter was enthusiastic about the Symphony when Dvořák first showed it to him in Vienna in November 1880 and asked to be allowed to give the first performance, which he envisaged to take place in his concert with the Philharmonic Society on 26 December. However, this première had to be postponed several times, presumably because of the then anti-Czech feeling in Vienna, and that is how Adolf Čech came to give the first performance in Prague.

to his unfortunate obsession: opera. Nevertheless he completed the Legends first and did not start sketching *Dimitrij* until 8 May, having first had consultations with the librettist, Marie Červinková-Riegrová. With how much conviction he set to work on this, one of his best operas, we do not know, but his singularity of purpose must certainly have been strengthened when Simrock accepted the 'Cunning Peasant' for publication at about that time, and in 1882 this became the first Dvořák opera to appear in print. Also, after a short summer holiday, the first of those Dvořák-Hanslick-Simrock meetings took place in Carlsbad in May 1881, and on 11 June the National Theatre was officially opened with Dvořák present.

Dvořák almost certainly would have wished for nothing more than to be allowed to work without interruption on his *Dimitrij*, but this was not to be. Apart from events which must have moved him deeply – the fire which destroyed the recently opened National Theatre on 12 August 1881 and the birth of his daughter Magdalena five days later – he was to have what must have come to him as a shock. Some time ago he had promised Hellmesberger a string quartet, and when Hellmesberger reminded him of this fact, he replied rather evasively that he was completely involved with *Dimitrij*. However, during another stay in Vysoká in October he did make an attempt and wrote an *Allegro vivace* for String Quartet in F, but he was not satisfied with it. As a result he discarded it – it now stands as an isolated Quartet Movement – and began composition on his String Quartet No. 11 in C (op.61). He had not even reached the Finale of this when the bombshell exploded: a press announcement in the early part of November stated that the Hellmesberger Quartet would play a new quartet by Dvořák on 15 December. A rude awakening indeed! But Dvořák coped, and by 10 November 1881 the work was finished. In the event, this particular concert had to be postponed because of the fire in the Vienna *Ringtheater*, and the first performance was given in Berlin on 2 November 1882 by the Joachim Quartet (not in Bonn on 6 December, as has been wrongly assumed until recently). It has already been mentioned that this quartet displays a certain classical severity, probably due to the fact that he wrote for the Viennese in a certain spirit of awe. But this does not mean that Dvořák abandoned his innate style, for the result is as beautiful and melodious a quartet as anyone could possibly wish for – it is just that his style was more than usually controlled. Only three more string quartets were to follow after this one in C major, all three dating from his American and post-American years.

Having completed this quartet Dvořák still could not get down to *Dimitrij*. He must have finished the first draft some time in early October 1881, but now the next job in hand was the orchestration of the Legends (which he completed by 9 December) and then he hoped to get on at long last with the opera. However, another proposition cropped up which Dvořák could not pass up so easily: a request to write an Overture and Incidental Music for a play by F. F. Šamberk, *Josef Kajetán Tyl*. Tyl, in a sense, was the father of Czech theatre, and for this reason Dvořák played strongly on Škroup's national song *Kde domov můj?* ('Where is my Home?'), the song which was later to become the Czech National Anthem. The Incidental Music is all but forgotten nowadays, but the Overture has become popular as a separate piece under the title 'My Home' (*Domov můj*). It is one of those ironies of fate that Simrock, in 1882, published this fervently patriotic piece under the German title *Mein Heim*. There is no record of Dvořák's reaction, but the Czech language is by no means deficient in lurid expletives . . .

He did not travel abroad a great deal during those years. Apart from short journeys within Bohemia, he only went to Vienna in November 1880 to show the score of his Symphony No.6 to Hans Richter, to Berlin in October 1881 to visit Joachim and from there on to Dresden to be present at Joachim's concert there on 20 October. Then, in February 1882, after a visit from von Bülow in Prague, Dvořák travelled to Leipzig – a trip which is of no intrinsic importance, except that he made the return journey from Leipzig to Prague in the company of his dear friend Johannes Brahms. From the early 1880s onwards, the number of performances of Dvořák's works becomes too numerous to be listed in detail. His music was rapidly becoming popular in many countries, as has been seen in the case of the Slavonic Rhapsody No. 3 and the *Stabat Mater.*

On 3 February 1882 the Overture and Incidental Music to *Josef Kajetán Tyl* had their first performance, and on the following day Dvořák left for Chrudim, where the opera 'The Old Bridegroom' by his friend Karel Bendl had its première. At that time Dvořák was already fully engaged on his *Dimitrij.* He had re-started work on the opera in January 1882, and until it was completed on 23 September virtually nothing else was allowed to intervene, although he did set five texts by the poet Vítězslav Hálek to music (for mixed chorus) under the title *V přírodě* ('In Nature's Realm', op.63) – not to be confused with the overture of the same name of 1891! He also paid a couple of visits to Göbl in Sychrov and made short trips to various friends (including Joachim in Berlin) but basically his life was dominated by *Dimitrij.* The opera had its first performance in Prague under the direction of Mořic Anger on 8 October 1882, and again we must marvel how, in those days, they managed to prepare a work for performance in such a short space of time. He revised the work in 1894/95 which shows the great importance which, quite rightly, he attached to this opera.

Immediately after this first performance Dvořák put the finishing touches to his Violin Concerto which he took with him on his visit to Joachim in Berlin. Joachim gave it a run-through in a rehearsal at the Berlin Conservatorium but, as has been said, the dedicatee never played the work in a public concert. Then Dvořák returned to Prague and composed a couple of songs and a work which is a curiosity in that it is Dvořák's shortest composition: an Album Leaf for a friend – *Otázka* ('Question') for piano – consisting of precisely eight bars.(See illustration 24)

On 8 December 1882 Dvořák was made an Honorary Member of the Society of Artists, which was a great honour for him. Sadly seven days later his mother died in Kladno. It was perhaps his deep sense of loss which inspired him early in 1883 to compose his Piano Trio in F minor (op.65). It is in four movements and strongly shows the influence of Brahms. There is hardly another work in Dvořák's output so sorrowful, sombre and poignant. It must rank amongst the greatest of Dvořák's chamber music compositions. This gloom was not even dispelled by the birth of a son, Antonín, on 7 March 1883 (his first son since Otakar, who had died at the age of three in 1877) nor does the news of the highly successful first English performance of his *Stabat Mater* in London a few days later seem to have cheered him up. He completed the F minor Trio on the last day of March 1883, and still the gloom persisted.

But wonderful are the ways of a composer's mind: only four days later, on 4 April, he began writing his *Scherzo capriccioso* (op.66), a work full of Bohemian charm and ebullience which keeps to the strict form of a symphonic Scherzo, though on a much larger scale. Here again we find one of Dvořák's favourite harmonic tricks in that it seems to start in B flat major before settling into the principal key of D flat major. The composer furthermore provides an element of surprise by giving us a second subject in the remote key of G. He completed the *Scherzo capriccioso* on 2 May 1883 and it had its first performance in Prague a matter of a mere two weeks later, again under the baton of Adolf Čech.

During June and July 1883 Dvořák 'commuted' between Prague and Vysoká, and at that time both *Vanda* and *Dimitrij* underwent some revision. But the greatest news came to him in August when he received an official invitation from the Philharmonic Society of London to come to England in March of the following year to conduct his own music. Not only was this a great honour for him, but it laid the real foundation for his international reputation and tied him in closely with a country he later came to love. However, before this historic first journey was to take place, other matters intervened. The director of the Prague National Theatre, František Adolf Šubert, had asked Dvořák to collaborate with him on a trilogy on the subject of Hus. Dvořák was enthusiastic. True, Šubert never got beyond the first act of the first part of the planned trilogy, but thanks to his intentions we now have Dvořák's 'Hussite Overture' (*Husitská*, op.67) In it he combined those two great Czech tunes, the Hussite Hymn and the St. Wenceslas Chorale, despite the fact that they are diametrically opposed, the one being Protestant, the other Catholic. But this did not disturb Dvořák greatly, for to him they were both expressions of the innate national spirit. However, other people took different views, some on religious grounds, some because they considered the Hussite Hymn a sort of private property of Smetana. Even outside the confines of the Czech Lands Hans von Bülow was criticized for his championship of this particular overture by the xenophobia of ultra-Germans. Nevertheless *Husitská* is a glorious piece of music and, despite its indirect underlying programme, the overture follows the basic precepts of sonata form. It is also a powerful work, and now that the squabbles regarding the linking of the two tunes have died down, it should appear far more often on the programmes of symphony concerts. By way of a dedication Dvořák wrote on the autograph: 'This overture was written by me for the re-opening of the National Theatre (after the fire in November 1883)' and, indeed, it had its first performance conducted by Mořic Anger at the festival matinée, held on the day of the re-opening of the National Theatre (18 November 1883).

Meanwhile Dvořák had been to Vienna again to visit Brahms who played him parts of his new Symphony No. 3 in F. The Violin Concerto had its first performce in Prague on 14 October 1883 with František Ondříček as soloist, and Dvořák worked on yet another cycle of six pieces for piano duet under the title of *Ze Šumavy* ('From the Bohemian Forest', op. 68) – just the sort of thing his publisher Simrock loved. Dvořák had great difficulty in finding titles, both for the cycle as a whole and for the individual pieces. He bitterly complained that

'Schumann had used up all the best ones', and in the event Marie Červinková-Riegrová came to his assistance and solved the problem for him. It should perhaps be mentioned in this connection that the fifth of these pieces, *Klid* ('Silent Woods'), he arranged for cello and orchestra in 1893. In addition *Dimitrij* received its first performance in a revised version at the National Theatre on 20 November, so that 1883 had indeed been a good year for Dvořák. His trip to Vienna in December was perhaps the crowning touch, for on the second day of that month he was present at a concert, conducted by Hans Richter, which included the première of Brahms' Symphony No 3 as well as the first performance in Vienna of his own Violin Concerto, again with Ondříček as soloist.

Despite all these successes, there were also outward adversities. Dvořák complained to Simrock about the level of his fees. Simrock in turn complained about the illegibility of Dvořák's manuscripts, and that large-scale works were difficult to sell; he wanted songs, short piano pieces and, if possible, Slavonic Dances (or the like) by the ream. This latter complaint was soon to stand Dvořák in good stead as we shall see, but for some time the relationship between composer and publisher was somewhat strained – even though Dvořák visited Simrock in the last days of January 1884 in Berlin while there to hear Brahms' Symphony No. 3 under the baton of the composer himself.

ACCLAIM IN ENGLAND

Dvořák's first visit to England was a triumphant success, and it is impossible to attribute too much importance to what England meant to his career as well as to him personally. He came to England nine times altogether, and it may perhaps be of interest to have a complete listing of his visits:

March 1884	London
September 1884	London, Worcester
April/May 1885	London
August 1885	London, Birmingham
October/November 1886	London, Leeds, Birmingham
April 1890	London
June 1891	Cambridge
October 1891	London, Birmingham
March 1896	London

The first of these trips he undertook with his friend, the pianist Jindřich Káan, leaving Prague on 5 March 1884 and travelling in easy stages via Nuremberg, Cologne, Brussels, Ostend and Dover. It can be imagined that Dvořák indulged in his hobby of engine-spotting to the fullest extent, and we are informed that he heaved a deep sigh of relief when, at Ostend, he found the channel as smooth as a mill-pond. For this was Dvořák's first view of the open sea, and he had been somewhat apprehensive of the channel crossing. It is amusing to note that Brahms was equally reluctant to travel far afield, especially by sea – so much so that he turned down the offer of an Honorary Doctorate from Cambridge University rather than undertake that same crossing!

London welcomed Dvořák enthusiastically. The pianist Oskar Beringer was his host, both Henry Littleton (sole owner of Novello, Ewer & Co.) and the Philharmonic Society gave banquets in his honour, and musicians greeted him with delight whenever he came to rehearsals. It is true that the way had been well paved for him by Hans Richter, Charles Hallé and August Manns, and the Slavonic Dances and Rhapsodies, the *Stabat Mater*, the Symphony in D and the Piano Concerto had all been heard. Similarly, Joseph Joachim had done his best to popularize Dvořák's chamber music by including the String Sextet in A and the Quartet in E flat in his programmes wherever he could. But in addition Dvořák's personality, that combination of simplicity, astuteness and sincerity together with his broken English, his beard and his firm handshake must have endeared him to one and all.

On this first visit Dvořák spent just over two weeks in London, 8 to 26 March 1884, but they must have been full of events. Apart from rehearsals he conducted three concerts. The Philharmonic Society had kindly allowed him to conduct his *Stabat Mater* at the Royal Albert Hall on 13 March, exactly one week before their own concert for which, officially, he had come to London, but they balked at allowing him to conduct a concert two days later, on 15 March, at which Joachim was to have been the soloist. It is a pity because, if this concert had come about, it might have been an occasion for Joachim to play Dvořák's Violin Concerto. The Philharmonic Society's own concert was on 20 March and included the *Husitská* Overture, the Symphony No. 6 in D and the Slavonic Rhapsody No. 2. On the following day Dvořák wrote to his father in Kladno:

'. . . Yesterday I had my second concert in St. James's Hall where I again achieved the most splendid success! I cannot tell you how great is the honour and respect the English people here show me. Everywhere they write and talk about me and say that I am the *lion* of this year's musical season in London! Two banquets have already been given in my honour, and on Monday, a third, and a very grand one, is being given by the society of artists, the "Philharmonia", which invited me to London. In September I shall have to come here again, but still farther to beyond London. It is the big industrial town of *Worcester* [sic], where I shall again conduct Stabat Mater. For next year and '86 I already have offers to come to England and shall have to write new compositions.'

One further appearance of Dvořák as a conductor was to follow in a concert at the Crystal Palace on 22 March, where the programme included the *Nokturno* as well as the first English performance of the *Scherzo capriccioso*. But perhaps the most important aspects of this visit were the invitations to Worcester, the enquiry from Leeds whether he would consider writing a sacred choral work for their 1886 Festival and, above all, his dealings with Littleton. Novello had accepted the *Hymnus* 'The Heirs of the White Mountain' for publication and had also commissioned a cantata from him (which later turned out to be the 'Spectre's Bride'). Dvořák demanded £200 for it, but subsequently Littleton paid £250. So all in all it was a somewhat tired Dvořák who returned to Prague on 29 March.

But it was also a happy Dvořák. Not only had he received the most wonderful ovations, not only could he feel that he had found a true foothold in England, but he also had in his pocket a contract to compose a cantata for Novello. Nevertheless, despite the exhaustion which he must have felt after the long journey and all the excitement, he was not allowed to relax. One week after returning to Prague he conducted *Dimitrij* at the National Theatre on 5 April 1884 and, on 6 and 7 April, two performances of the *Stabat Mater* in Pilsen (Plzeň). Then he took part as pianist in a concert of his works in Prague, and 26/27 April saw him in Olomouc (Olmütz) for further performances of the *Stabat Mater*. It was only early in May that he found time for a holiday in his beloved Vysoká, where he first completed the final revision of his *Hymnus* 'The Heirs of the White Mountain', and then he settled down to writing something in order to fulfil his new commission from Littleton.

At this point we must revert to the more personal aspects of Dvořák's life. As will be remembered, his first great love had been Josefina Čermáková, who jilted him, and whose sister Anna Dvořák later married. Josefina had, in turn, married Count Kaunic who had his country estate in Vysoká near the mining town of Příbram. During the years 1880-84 Dvořák was a frequent visitor to the Kaunic estate, having there what was euphemistically called the 'Forest Lodge' (a barn made just about habitable) placed at his disposal. It was here that he had composed many works and wrote large parts of the 'Spectre's Bride'. In Vysoká he re-discovered his love for nature, his need for the calm of the countryside. It now became his greatest ambition to have a second home in the country. The 3500 Marks which Simrock paid him for *Husitská* and *Ze Šumavy* plus his earnings in England allowed him to contemplate such a project, and from his brother-in-law Count Kaunic he acquired a plot of land in Vysoká.

In various books this 'plot of land' has been referred to as a 'sheep run', a 'barn', or a 'shepherd's hut'. In order to get some clarity into the matter, I would like to quote from a letter (the original is in German) which Dr. Karel Mikysa, Secretary of the Antonín Dvořák Society and Director (retired) of the Antonín Dvořák Museum of Prague, wrote to me on 3 March 1979:

'The country house N.C.16 at Vysoká near Příbram:
This house was originally an old sheep stable which, together with the surrounding grounds, belonged to the Vysoká estate. The owner of this estate – Dvořák's brother-in-law Dr. Václav Count Kaunic – sold this sheep stable as well as the grounds for a low price to Dvořák in 1884. Dvořák, with the help of Count Kaunic (materials as well as labour) had this sheep stable rebuilt, and turned the surrounding grounds into a garden with many trees,

which he received from the estates of Vysoká as well as Sychrov. . . . The expense of this undertaking, which cannot have been exorbitant, Dvořák defrayed from his publishers' (Simrock, Novello) and conductor's fees (England).

In later years this country house was called "Rusalka" or "Villa Rusalka" by Dvořák's son-in-law Josef Suk.

In the forests around Vysoká there is a mere which, in 1954, was named "Little Lake of Rusalka" (*Rusalčino Jezírko*) by the Antonín Dvořák Society of Prague.'

By October 1884 the house was ready. Dvořák could move in, and from then onwards for the rest of his life, apart from those times when he was travelling, he simply spent the summer months in Vysoká and the winters in Prague. The so-called 'Forest Lodge' was destroyed by fire in 1972, but 'Villa Rusalka' is still in the possession of Dvořák's descendants and is used as a weekend house, although the major part of it has been turned into a museum.

Unfortunately Dvořák had difficulties in finding a suitable libretto for the cantata or oratorio which Littleton had commissioned, and in the end he turned to a ballad by K. J. Erben who specialized in Czech folklore. The poem of his choice was *Svatební košile*, which literally means 'The Bridal Shirt'. The story is very similar to Bürger's famous ballad *Leonore*: that of an orphaned girl whose lover has been away for many years. She prays for his return, and return he *does* – but unbeknown to her he has died and is but a ghost. He leads her through wild countryside, ostensibly to take her to his family mansion, which turns out to be a graveyard. Unlike in Bürger's grisly version, however, the heroine in the end finds salvation in prayer. This sort of story may have sent pleasurable shivers down the spines of our grandfathers and great-grandfathers; to our present-day mentality, it is apt only to make us feel slightly embarrassed. (Personally I find that a performance using the Czech language, with its peculiar

HOSPODINE, POMILUJ NY!

Ho - spo - di - ne, po - mi - luj ny, Je - zu - kri - ste, po - mi - luj
ny, spa - se vše - ho mi - ra, spa-siž ny i u - slyš, Ho - spo - di - ne, hla - sy na-
aj nám všěm, Ho - spo - di - ne, žizn a mír v ze - mi! Kr - leš! Kr - leš! Kr - l

SVATÝ VÁCLAVE

1. Sva - tý Vá - cla - ve, vé - vo - do Če - ské ze - mě, kně - že
ros ža ny Bo - ha, sva - té - ho Du - cha! Kri - ste - le - y - son!

KTOŽ JSÚ BOŽÍ BOJOVNÍCI

1. Ktož jsú bo - ží bo - jo-vní - ci   a zá - ko - na je - ho,   pro - ste od Bo - ha po-mo-
Kri-stus†vám za ško-dy sto - jí,   sto-krát viec sli - bu - je,   pak - li kto proň ži-vot slo -
a ú - faj-te v ně - ho,   že ko - ne-čně vždy - cky s ním sví - tě - zí - te.   R° Tenť Pán ve-
vě - čný mie-ti bu - de,   bla - ze kaž-dé - mu, ktož na pra-vdě sen - de.
se ne - bá - ti zá - hub-cí tě - les - ných,   ve-lí† i ži - vot slo - ži - ti   pro lá - sku svých bliž-n

1 The three great Czech tunes: the *Hospodine*, the St. Wenceslas
  Chorale, and the Hussite Hymn

2 Nelahozeves (16th century engraving)

3 Dvořák's father, František and
his sister Josefina Dušková

4 Dvořák's birth house in
Nelahozeves

5 The church of Nelahozeves
opposite Dvořák's birth house

6 The 16th century font in which
Dvořák was baptized

7 The *Big Inn* in Zlonice

'The Bells of Zlonice'

9 The old school house in Zlonice

10 Anton Liehmann

11 The Organ School in the
Old Town of Prague

12 St. Adalbert's Church

Dvořák in 1865

14 Anna Čermáková,
Dvořák's wife-to-be

15 Josefina and Anna Čermáková
in their teens (Anna at the pianino)

6 Jean Becker

7 Joseph Joachim

18 František Ondříček

19 The house in Na Rybníčku No.14   20 The house at Žitná No.10

21 Dvořák's music room, Žitná No.10

22 Smetana surrounded by the members of
the National Theatre Orchestra (1870).
(Dvořák in the second row, third from left)

23 Bedřich Smetàna

24 Dvořák's shortest composition:
Otázka ('Question')

25 Sketch of Version I of the Violin
Concerto

26 Johannes Brahms in 1878

27 Fritz Simrock

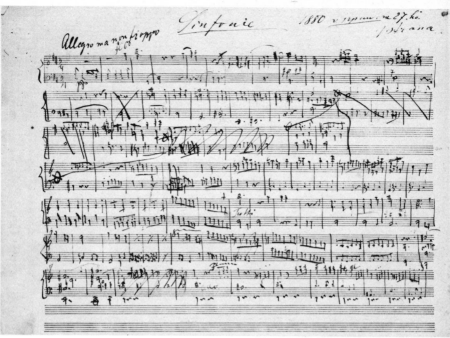

28 Sketch for Symphony No.6

29 Autograph title page of Symphony No.7

"Vysoká" 10 of September 85.

My dear friend!

I am arrived quite well
in my home.
The worry worry days of Birmingham were
at once and now they
again quite alone as before.
Daily your walking in
the beautiful forests and
reflecting about Ludmila.
Many thanks for the
reviewing Coppys ch
the Oratorio's and Cantatas.
The Editor of the Graphic
in London asked me
for my Portrait.

but I am sorry, not
to have one.

Please will you be so kind
and send him an photograps
from Birmingham, they
supposed they are ready.

Another time something
more.

My best complimentsto
your family.

God bye
Yours
... sincerely
Ant. Dvořák

1 Karel Bendl

32 Alois Göbl

Leoš Janáček

34 Photo which Josef Suk sent, with a dedication, to Otilie in New York

THE
SPECTRE'S BRIDE

(Die Geisterbraut)   (Svatební košile)

A dramatic Cantata
written by
K. J. Erben
The music composed
For Soli, Chorus and Orchestra
by
ANTONÍN DVOŘÁK
Op.69.

Orchestral parts.   Full score.

London & New York
NOVELLO, EWER & Cọ

*Psáno pro
festival v Birming-
ham 1885.
(26 srpna
8.*

*Tuto skladbu jsem poprvé řídil
řídil v Plzni, kteby skladatel na zpra skotem
Hlaholem, v březnu   1885.*

Antonín Dvořák

5 Title page of 'The Spectre's Bride'

36 Dvořák in 1876

37 Dvořák in 1891 after
receiving his Honorary
Doctorate in Cambridge

38 Dvořák's house in Vysoká

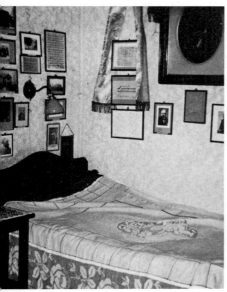

39 Dvořák's bed in Vysoká

40 The Garden Pavillion in Vysoká

41 Dvořák with his wife Anna in London,
1886

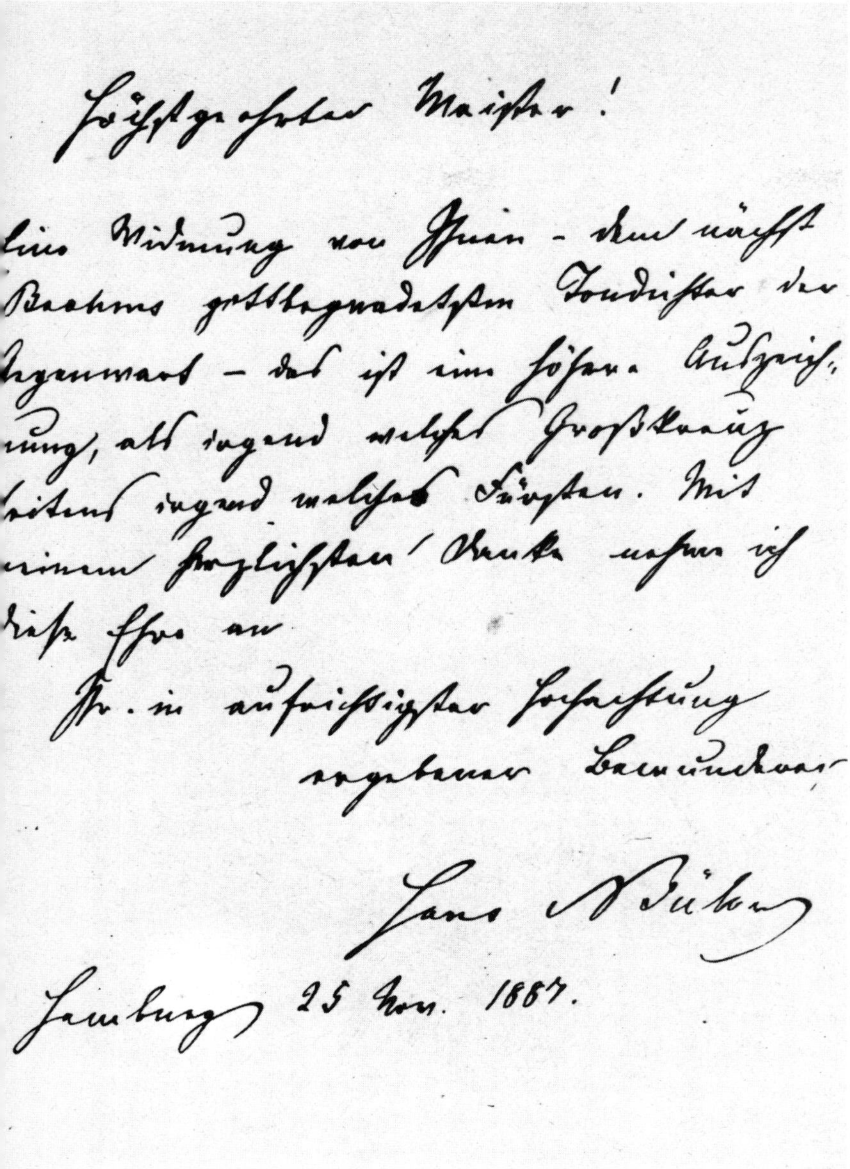

Hochgeehrter Meister!

Eine Widmung von Ihnen – dem nächst
Brahms gottbegnadetsten Tondichter der
Gegenwart – das ist eine höhere Auszeich-
nung, als irgend welches Grosskreuz
seitens irgend welches Fürsten. Mit
meinem herzlichsten Danke nehme ich
diese Ehre an

Ihr in aufrichtigster Hochachtung
ergebener Bewunderer

Hans Bülow

Hamburg 25 Nov. 1887.

Letter from Hans von Bülow to Dvořák

43 Photo of Tchaikovsky with a dedication
   to Dvořák

Dvořák in Vysoká with his pigeons

Locomotives in Dvořák's days

46 S.S. Saale

47 Dvořák's passport

48 Press notice in the New York
Times of 16 October 1892

Dvořák in New York, 1893

50 Dvořák's home in New York,
327 E 17th Street

Mrs. Jeanette Thurber

52 The house where the Dvořák family lived in Spillville during their summer holiday in 1893

53 Sketch for the Finale of the String Quartet in F

An early sketch for the second movement of the 'New World' Symphony

First sketches for the Cello Concerto

56 Jaroslav Kvapil

57 A group of Czech composers (Left to right: K. Bendl, Dvořák, J.B. Foerster, J. Káan, K. Kovařovic, Z. Fibich)

Hans Richter

59 Hans von Bülow

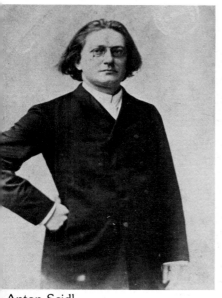

Anton Seidl

61 Arthur Nikisch

62 A family group taken by Dvořák's son Otakar, c.1901.
(From left to right: back row, daughter Anna, a friend, daughter Magda;
middle row, Dvořák's sister-in-law T. Koutecká, Dvořák, wife Anna;
front row, daughter Aloisie, son Antonín, a friend).

63 Dvořák's children
(left to right) Antonín, Magda, Aloisie and Otakar in Vysoká, 1951

The grave of Dvořák's father
in Velvary

The National Theatre in 1974

66 Dvořák's tomb on Vyšerad

67 The Antonín Dvořák Museum, Prague

richness, enhances my enjoyment of Dvořák's music!)

The English text of *Svatební košile* (op.69) was supplied by that ineffable Victorian, the Rev. John Troutbeck, whose susceptibilities were shocked to the core that something as vulgar as a shirt should be mentioned in the title of a cantata. This he rendered as 'The Spectre's Bride'. Under this title the work has been known in English ever since and similarly in German as *Die Geisterbraut*. Dvořák started on the first sketches in May 1884, began the full score in July and worked on it without interruption until the end of August, when he had to leave for England again.

The only event of importance which falls into that period was Dvořák's election as an Honorary Member of the Philharmonic Society of London (not 'Royal Philharmonic Society' as some authorities will have it – the prefix 'Royal' was only granted by charter in 1912). Of course it was tacitly implied that the conferment of such an honour would oblige the composer to write a major instrumental work for the Society, but then, again, we know that in fact Dvořák had already agreed to write a new symphony for the Philharmonic Society before leaving London in March 1884.

His second visit to England, 1-14 September 1884, was due to an invitation from the Three Choirs Festival, which in that year took place at Worcester. In London he stayed with Henry Littleton and then went on to Worcester where, on 11 September 1884, he conducted his *Stabat Mater* in the Cathedral in the morning and a concert including the Symphony in D in the evening. Three days later he was on his return journey, yet despite rehearsals and concerts it must have been during those days in England that he also wrote a *Dumka* and a *Furiant* for piano (both subsequently published as op.12!). How enthusiastically Dvořák was again greeted in England is best gauged from a letter which he wrote to his wife Anna on the day after the performances:

'. . . Everywhere I appear, whether in the street or at home or even when I go into a shop to buy something, people crowd round me and ask for my autograph. There are pictures of me at all the booksellers and people buy them only to have some memento.'

After his return to Vysoká on 16 September 1884 Dvořák had two relatively quiet months – apart from the move into the country house – during which he could devote all his time to the 'Spectre's Bride' and eventually completed it on 27 November. The only interruptions were a concert in Prague, where he conducted his Symphony in D, and a brief trip to Berlin where, on 21 November, he appeared for the first time as a conductor. The programme included the Overture *Husitská* and the Piano Concerto in G minor (with Anna Grosser-Rilke as soloist) and not the Berlin première of the Symphony No. 6, as some authorities claim. Presumably in Berlin he also met up with Simrock again, and this meeting must have been somewhat difficult for him, as Simrock could not be allowed to know of the negotiations with Novello. But then, Dvořák always could use as an excuse Simrock's eternal complaints that large-scale works 'did not sell'.

Back at home, and with the 'Spectre's Bride' finally completed, he had to conduct the *Stabat Mater* again in Prague and Pilsen. There was also a visit to Prague of the Meiningen Orchestra under Hans von Bülow, who included Dvořák's Overture *Domov můj* in their Prague concert on 4 December 1884, and von Bülow generously invited the composer to conduct this overture himself. Otherwise nothing was to disturb him in his work until late March 1885 when, on 28 March, he had to conduct the first performance of 'The Spectre's Bride' in Pilsen. However, a happy family event also falls into that period: another child was born to Anna and Antonín on 9 February 1885, another boy. After the loss of their first three children, the Dvořáks now had five children around them again, and this newest arrival was christened Otakar – the name of their very first child who had died at the age of three.

From 13 December 1884 until March 1885 Dvořák worked with utter singularity of purpose. Ever since Brahms had played him excerpts of his own Symphony in F in Vienna more than a year ago, thoughts of a new symphony had been going through Dvořák's mind. Moreover there was that promise to the Philharmonic Society of London to write a new symphony for them and so, during those three months, the Symphony No. 7 in D minor (op.70) – the only time within the canon of his nine symphonies that Dvořák repeated himself in tonality, for Symphony No. 4 had also been in D minor – came into being in one uninterrupted flow of inspiration. With Brahms' latest symphony and the honours bestowed on him by London in his mind, it is not surprising that Dvořák felt himself obliged to create something special, something outstanding: '. . . [it] must be capable of shaking the world . . .' In the resultant Symphony we encounter Dvořák at his nearest to the symphonic concept of Brahms, at his concisest, but of all his symphonies it is also the one which is painted in only sombre colours. This sombreness is not even relieved by the third movement which, whilst entitled *Scherzo*, is really a *Furiant* – though in 6/4 time instead of the customary 3/4. Nor is the issue greatly affected by the argument that the Finale, which basically adheres to the minor mode, changes into the major in the last few bars: this is merely a judicious use of the *Tierce de Picardie** and not a sort of expression of ultimate victory such as we find in Beethoven's Fifth. It is not surprising, therefore, that initially audiences were not quite as enthusiastic as usual, for they were accustomed to getting music from Dvořák which was full of sunshine and Bohemian melodies. Nevertheless, eventually the symphony made its impact and now vies in popularity with his two last works in this form.

What was the reason for this apparent despondency? Some writers maintain that it still reflects his sorrow over the death of his mother, but I am far more inclined to agree with Šourek and Clapham that it marks the end of a crisis in Dvořák's emotional life: he had not succeeded in his ambition

*This term is applied to a major third used at the end of a composition which is otherwise in a minor key, thus converting the expected minor close into the major.

to become a truly successful composer of operas. The reasons for this failure to become acknowledged in that particular field have already been amply discussed, and also the fact that publishers, directors of opera houses and the like had been pestering him for some time to compose an opera on the basis of a German libretto with a less nationally-orientated plot. For many years Dvořák had wavered, but then he came to the momentous decision to stick to his guns. The Symphony in D minor is like a final rearing-up against the adversities of destiny.

A week or so after completing the symphony Dvořák went to Pilsen to conduct the première of the 'Spectre's Bride', then back to Prague, and a fortnight later he was on his way again to England. On his first English journey he had the pianist Jindřich Káan as his travel companion, for his second visit he had asked the journalist and critic V.J. Novotný to accompany him and now, on his third trip to London, he had asked Dr. Josef Zubatý, a Professor of the Czech Language, to come with him. The two men arrived in London on 19 April 1885, and this time Dvořák stayed in England for about four weeks as the guest of Henry Littleton. His first conducting engagement was to give the first performance of the D minor Symphony at St. James's Hall, London, on 22 April 1885 at a concert of the Philharmonic Society to whom the work is dedicated. The reception of this new symphony, though well received, was not as enthusiastic as that of his Symphony No. 6 a year or so earlier, and the reaction in the press was also somewhat mixed.

While in London Dvořák fulfilled other conducting engagements, such as accompanying the pianist Franz Rummel in the G minor Piano Concerto and giving the first performance of his *Hymnus* 'The Heirs of the White Mountain' in its third and final version, but the length of his stay gave him enough time to enjoy London. He went to the theatre, took strolls in Hyde Park and Regent's Park, visited the Royal Society of

Musicians, and made contact with many composers. In between he also composed two charming songs, strangely enough to German translations of Czech folk-poems – to my knowledge the only time that he ever did such an 'unpatriotic' thing.

Two days after returning from London, Dvořák went to the country, to Vysoká, where he spent virtually the whole summer, from mid-May until mid-August. The only major journey was the trip to Carlsbad for the Simrock-Hanslick meeting, which was a strained affair, but Dvořák was able to make his points – particularly as far as the fee he expected for the D minor Symphony was concerned – with some measure of success. For the rest of it he took life fairly easily, occupying himself only with minor alterations to his Symphony No. 7 and some further revision of the score of *Dimitrij*. The other event worth reporting is that towards the end of that summer Dvořák at long last found a suitable text for the national oratorio which he longed to write: a libretto by the poet and novelist Jaroslav Vrchlický on the subject of Saint Ludmila. But before he could even envisage beginning to sketch the work, he had to go to England again.

This was his fourth visit to England, and it was the first time that he undertook the journey by himself. He left Bohemia on 15 August 1885 and arrived in London on 17 August, the main purpose of the trip being to conduct the first English performance of 'The Spectre's Bride' at the Birmingham Musical Festival on 27 August. This time he only stayed in England for about eleven days, and his time-table must have been absolutely hectic, for in those days Birmingham did not yet boast an orchestra of its own, which meant that Dvořák had to double backwards and forwards, taking choral rehearsals in Birmingham and orchestral rehearsals in London. How he managed to find the time to spend a day in Brighton with Littleton is a mystery! But the performance of 'The Spectre's Bride' was a huge success – so much so that Leeds invited him to provide an oratorio for their festival the following year. On the very day after that Birmingham performance Dvořák was on his return journey and arrived safely at home in Vysoká on 31 August.

Back at home, Dvořák wrote a letter to his friend and publisher Henry Littleton, which intrinsically is of no importance except that he wrote it in English, and the following literal reproduction of the text gives such a lovely idea of the stage which Dvořák's knowledge of the English language had reached by then:

'My dear friend,
    I am arrived quite well in my home.
    The verry merry days of Birmingham ar over and naw stay I agin quiet alone as before. Daily I am walking in the beutyful forestes and reflecting about Ludmila. Many thanks for the revieving Coppys of the Oratoris and Cantatas.
    The Editor of the Graphic in London asked me for my Portrait, but I am sorry, not to have one.
    Please will you be so kind and send him an photography from Birmingham, supposed they are ready.
    Another time something more.
    My best compliments fo your family.
                                    God bye, yours sincerely
                                            Ant. Dvořák.'

There is little to tell of that winter of 1885/86 which in the main Dvořák spent in Prague with occasional breaks in Vysoká. Performances of his music became more and more frequent and his 'Spectre's Bride' was heard as far afield as Milwaukee. In Prague *Dimitrij* had its first performance at the National Theatre in the first revised version on 28 November 1885, and the following day Dvořák himself conducted his Symphony in D minor at the Rudolfinum (now the *Dům Umělců*, the 'House of Artists'). The fiasco of the Vienna performance of the 'Cunning Peasant' in November 1885 has already been referred to, and during the first months of 1886 London heard the 'Spectre's Bride' and the Violin Concerto for the first time. Of course during that time Dvořák had to be present at performances of his music in Prague, but otherwise he concentrated entirely on his oratorio *Svatá Ludmila* ('St. Ludmila'). He began the sketch of Part I in Vysoká on 17 September 1885 and worked on it steadily until the sketch was finished on 23 November. The score of Part I Dvořák concluded on 18 January 1886, and he followed the same plan with Parts II and III, first sketching each section and then completing it before going on to the next. By 30 May 1886 the whole score was finished.

Perhaps it is as well at this juncture to clear up a misconception which is widely disseminated in the literature on Dvořák as regards the £2000 which he reputedly received from Novello for this oratorio. It is hardly feasible even to suppose that a publishing firm should pay such an enormous fee – by the standard of monetary values of the 1880s – and I shall give verbatim the conclusions reached by John Clapham in his research:

> 'Much attention has been given to the belief that Littleton offered Dvořák £2000 for his oratorio (*St. Ludmila*). It is curious, however, that he should have been ready to pay ten times as much as the composer demanded in return for the publishing and performing rights in all countries for his cantata (*The Spectre's Bride*). The truth is that no sum of money was agreed to during Dvořák's visit, and the first mention of the need to settle terms does not occur in the correspondence until almost two years later. Dvořák hoped to receive £1000, whereas Littleton had been expecting to pay £500. They finally compromised at £650, on 20 February 1886, with the proviso that if the composer proved to be right in thinking his work would be a great success, Littleton would give him an additional £350. In his letter to the publisher, Dvořák commented (in English): "I believe your proposal is for you and me a very fine one." '*

*John Clapham, *Dvořák* (David & Charles, London 1978) p.64.

For eight and a half months all Dvořák's energies were directed towards the completion of 'St. Ludmila', and at times he nearly despaired, thinking the score would never get finished in time. Now it was safely on its way to England, and he had to turn to other things. Having extracted the noble sum of 6000 Marks from Simrock at their meeting in Carlsbad in April 1885 for his Symphony No. 7, he now felt obliged to redeem his own promise and write a second set of eight Slavonic Dances. As with the earlier set, he first wrote them for piano duet and it took him just over a month to compose them. But whereas the first set was based (with one single exception) on Bohemian dances only, the second set also included dances of Ukranian, Slovak, Polish and Serbian origin. For some reason this second set of Slavonic Dances never seems to have caught the public imagination as much as the first, even though these second eight are by no means inferior. Perhaps the main reason lies in the fact that Dvořák's music is so much associated in people's minds with Bohemian and Moravian tunes that they are somewhat estranged when he roams further afield in the realm of Slav music. In any case he could not immediately settle down to orchestrating them, for by then it was time to go to England again.

Dvořák left Prague on 1 October 1886, went to London and then on to Leeds. It was his fifth visit to England within the short space of two and a half years, and whereas on the first three occasions he was accompanied by friends and travelled by himself on the fourth, this time he took his wife Anna with him. According to Gervaise Hughes the weather, even by English standards, was singularly inclement, so that they reduced their stay to a bare minimum.

Their base was once again the home of Henry Littleton in Sydenham, and Dvořák was as busy as ever. First there was the première of 'St. Ludmila' at the Leeds Music Festival on 15 October 1886, then there was yet another performance of the Symphony in D in Birmingham under Dvořák's own baton, and 'St. Ludmila' had two further performances, though in slightly abridged form, in London, with Dvořák conducting, and a performance of 'The Spectre's Bride' sandwiched in between. Yet, despite all rehearsals and performances, it appears that from Birmingham they still found time for an excursion to Stratford-on-Avon.

According to Dvořák's own letters and contemporary reports 'St. Ludmila' was acclaimed most enthusiastically, but some critics compared the oratorio unfavourably with 'The Spectre's Bride' – just as some time later they compared the *Requiem* unfavourably with 'St. Ludmila'. As usual, the critics were wrong on both occasions. Just as an amusing aside it might be mentioned that, while Dvořák was in London, 'The Spectre's Bride' received its Australian debut in Melbourne.

This might be a good moment to have a general look at Dvořák's output in the field of secular choral music. In all he wrote four major choral works unrelated to religious service: the *Hymnus* 'The Heirs of the White Mountain', 'The Spectre's Bride', 'St. Ludmila', and *The American Flag*. The last of these we can dispense with for the time being, as all there is to be said about it will be said when we come to Dvořák's years in America. The other three were successful in their time, and it must never be forgotten that with the *Hymnus* Dvořák first made his mark as a composer. But it is an early work, and despite its genuinely patriotic fervour it cannot transcend its period. Both the other oratorios suffer, though in different ways, from their librettos. The case of 'The Spectre's Bride' has already been examined. With 'St. Ludmila' we have to contend with a different problem. The story deals with the life of Ludmila, the wife of a Bohemian Duke, a Christian martyr, grandmother of St. Wenceslas, and Patron Saint of Bohemia. As a work it is unduly protracted and tends to get tedious even though, as ever with Dvořák, it contains much beautiful music. During its composition Dvořák undoubtedly had the Handelian tradition in mind, for some of the strongest sections of the oratorio are its enormous choral movements, particularly the great chorus which starts off Part III, based on the *Hospodine, pomiluj ny!* Dvořák seems also to have remembered Mozart's *Zauberflöte* – shades of Sarastro and the famous threefold chord. But the fact remains that in the 20th century we no longer have the patience to sit through oratorios lasting what seems an eternity – a capacity which apparently our Victorian ancestors *did* have. The fault does not lie with Dvořák and his music. With a change in the taste of the times the neglect of his oratorios is a fate which is shared by many similar works of other 19th century composers such as Schumann and Mendelssohn of whom Dvořák is an undisputed equal.

By 9 November 1886 Dvořák and his wife were back in Prague, and he was facing a task which he disliked intensely, namely the orchestration of his second set of Slavonic Dances. Simrock had been pressing him for this orchestration, and it is evident from the corespondence that the work was nothing but a chore to him. This distaste for the job is equally evident from the fact that it took him about two months to complete it – for Dvořák, the skilled orchestrator, an unconscionably long time. Nevertheless, the next day after the set was completed, Dvořák himself gave the first performance of three of them (Nos. 1, 2 and 7) in Prague.

The years 1887-89 Dvořák basically spent at home in his Bohemia, apart from a few trips of short duration to Berlin, Vienna and Budapest. He was free from all the shackles of regular jobs or appointments and could devote himself entirely to composition and to conducting his own works. As usual, having put the onerous job of orchestrating the second set of Slavonic Dances behind him, he turned to small-scale pieces and to delving into his earlier compositions. The first work to be written in January 1887 in the short space of one week was a four-movement *Terzetto* (op.74) for the unusual combination of two violins and viola. He was so pleased with this little work – and it is charming, though at times one misses the bass line which could have been provided by a cello – that he followed it up with a second work in the same genre which he entitled

Drobnosti ('Miniatures'). However, he never got beyond sketching it and then changed his mind: using the same thematic material, he altered it and turned it into four Romantic Pieces (op.75) for violin and piano. It was also during this time, when Dvořák was writing chamber music trifles, that Hans Richter scored a resounding success with the greatly delayed Viennese first performance of the D minor Symphony.

It is hardly significant that Dvořák once again dug out his 'King and Charcoal Burner' and subjected the third act to a thorough revision in February and March: some failures are simply beyond redemption. But a new impulse was to come, which gave Dvořák a creative incentive. An architect, the first president of the Czech Academy of Sciences and Arts, Josef Hlávka, who owned a country estate at Lužany, asked Dvořák to write a Mass for the consecration of his Chapel and so, between 26 March and 17 June 1887, the Mass in D (op.86) came into being. As it was intended for a private and intimate occasion, Dvořák composed it for choir and soloists with organ accompaniment only, and the first performance took place in the Lužany Chapel on 11 September 1887 with Dvořák himself conducting and his wife Anna as the solo alto. The Mass, if not Dvořák's greatest sacred work, is nonetheless typical, for it combines the liturgical with Bohemian musical elements and proclaims the fact that religious belief and the praise of God should also be a joyous affair. Needless to say, Simrock was not interested in the work, and so eventually Dvořák sold it to Novello. They, however, insisted on something on a larger scale, so Dvořák orchestrated the Mass between 24 March and 15 June 1892. Unfortunately, in the process of the orchestration the Mass lost something of the intimate atmosphere which must have pervaded the chapel at Lužany.

Work on the Mass was only interrupted by some conducting engagements, among them a concert in Vienna in which he accompanied Ondříček in a performance of the Violin Concerto, and – perhaps as a matter of relaxation – he scored twelve of his early songs 'Cypresses' for string quartet. But more important is the fact that, in March and April of that year 1887, he corresponded with Hans Richter and drew the latter's attention to the Symphonic Variations. Richter was enthusiastic about the work, and it seems incredible to us now that Dvořák had let it lie in a drawer for close on ten years, for it is undoubtedly one of Dvořák's finest and most original orchestral compositions. Richter gave the English première of these Variations in London in May 1887 and invited Dvořák to stay with him in Vienna for a few days in November. Less than a month later, in early December, Dvořák was back in Vienna to hear Richter conduct the Viennese first performance of the Symphonic Variations, and at the same time to visit his friend Brahms. Years later, when Hans Richter was the conductor of the Hallé Orchestra in Manchester (1900-1911) the Symphonic Variations continued to belong to his standard repertoire and were heard in almost every concert season.

The months between the completion of the Mass in D and his visit to Richter in Vienna were mainly spent in revision of his earlier compositions, particularly the 149th Psalm of 1879 which, in its first version, was for male chorus only. He made quite a few changes in the work, but the main difference is that he now replaced the male voices by a mixed chorus. The musical worth of this Psalm is no less than that of many other Dvořák compositions. With its predominant C major it proclaims the praise of Jehovah in no uncertain terms, but it shares the fate of many fine settings of psalms by other composers: they never seem to make a permanent place for themselves in the general repertoire. Is it because, as a rule, they are too long and too short for balanced programme building?

But another great composition – by some considered the greatest chamber work he ever wrote – was born during that period: the Piano Quintet in A (op.81). It certainly must rank amongst the finest works in this medium by any standards and can bear comparison with the piano quintets of Schubert, Schumann and Brahms. Originally he had attempted to revise his early Piano Quintet, also in A, of 1872, but this proved a hopeless undertaking. So he wrote an entirely new work which, though cast in the mould of the great classical tradition, gives free rein to his Slavonic temperament and is unashamedly nationalistic with its *Dumka* and its *Furiant* Scherzo, coupled with that interchanging between the major and minor modes which is such a peculiar characteristic of all Bohemian music. One cannot improve on what John Clapham has to say about it:

> 'This work probably epitomizes more completely the genuine Dvořák style in most of its facets than any other work of his. Laughter and tears, sorrow and gaiety, are found side by side, as well as many moods that lie between these two extremes. All are presented with consummate mastery, they are decked in a wide range of instrumental colouring, and through the whole sweeps the life-blood of vital rhythm.'

One thing is certain: among all his chamber music, this Piano Quintet is only rivalled in popularity by his *Dumky* Trio and the 'American' Quartet.

In October 1887, shortly after completing the Piano Quintet, Dvořák went to Berlin again to see Simrock and sold him the F major Symphony and the String Quintet in G of 1875, the 149th Psalm, and the Piano Quintet for a sizeable sum. The meeting between the two men seems to have been more cordial this time, and it may also have been on this occasion that Simrock gave in over the wretched argument as to the spelling of Dvořák's Christian name. But the hatchet was only partially buried, and three years later they severed relations completely for over a year.

On his return to Prague, and apparently undaunted by his earlier lack of success in this field, Dvořák's thoughts turned once again to opera. This time he wanted it to be a comedy subject, and after considering a variety of possibilities he settled on *Jacobín* ('The Jacobin') by Marie Červinková-Riegrová who had already furnished him with the libretto for

Dimitrij. On 10 November 1887, two days before he left to visit Richter in Vienna, he set to work on this, his seventh opera and worked on it with very few interruptions for a whole year until it was completed on 18 November 1888, although he still made some revisions in 1897. The first performance took place on 12 February 1889 at the National Theatre in Prague with Adolf Čech conducting. It was an unqualified success, but performances outside the Slavonic countries have remained rarities up to the present day. This is much to be regretted, for *Jacobín* is without doubt the most 'Bohemian' opera Dvořák ever composed. To anyone who knows Nelahozeves and its surroundings there can be no doubt that scenes from his childhood were before Dvořák's eyes in the first two acts which are set, respectively, in the market square of a small country town and in the house of the schoolmaster Benda. He must have visualized his father's *Gasthaus-Metzgerei* facing the church, and the whole opera is a glorification of a Bohemian village and those schoolmasters who did so much to lay the solid foundation of Czech music making. It makes one feel slightly ashamed to find out that the opera had its first German performance in Mannheim in 1941, and was not heard in Great Britain before 22 July 1947 (London, St. George's Hall).

During those twelve months Dvořák had virtually no other thought in his head except his opera. True, in December 1887 he wrote four songs, revised some earlier compositions in January 1888, and he also had to fulfil certain conducting engagements, including a performance of the *Stabat Mater* in Budapest in March 1888. The only other interruptions were a visit to Brno where his 'Spectre's Bride' was conducted by none other than his friend Leoš Janáček and, on 4 April 1888, the birth of his last child, daughter Aloisie (known in the family as Zinda) – if that can be termed an interruption. The year 1888 also marks the beginning of Dvořák's friendship with Tchaikovsky, who came to Prague for the first time in February 1888, when the two men met and spent some time together. Tchaikovsky returned to Prague on 27 November, nine days after the *Jacobín* had been completed, to conduct his own Symphony No. 5 and a performance of *Eugene Onegin*. Dvořák and Tchaikovsky remained firm friends until Tchaikovsky's death in 1893, and it is somewhat amusing that these two, who are among the greatest Slav composers, when writing to each other had to use German to make themselves understood: Dvořák could not read Russian, and Tchaikovsky could not read Czech. On the rare occasions when the two men exchanged letters in their mother tongues, this invariably led to delays, as can be seen from a passage in a letter from Tchaikovsky to Dvořák in January 1889:

> 'Forgive me for not answering your letter immediately. In spite of all my efforts to read your letter I could not understand it although I guessed that its contents were agreeable. The letter had to be sent to Moscow . . . to be translated and the translation only reached me today.'

England did not see Dvořák during 1888 – in fact did not see him again until April 1890 – but his name was kept fresh by Hans Richter, August Manns and Charles Hallé who continued to perform his music in London, Birmingham and Manchester.

After Tchaikovsky had left Prague in early December 1888, Dvořák took the 'Cypresses' of 1865 out of the drawer again and reworked eight of them as a cycle, 'Love Songs' (op.83). He must have had a particular fondness for these early songs, for he kept returning to them at intervals, either re-arranging them or using material from them in other works. But after this short song cycle we now come to one of the longest periods of barrenness in the whole of Dvořák's life as a composer. It lasted from December 1888 until mid-April 1889, and then initially only brought forth a set of thirteen piano pieces under the title 'Poetic Tone Pictures' (op.85). They are not amongst the best of Dvořák's works for piano and do not stand comparison with the earlier Waltzes or the later Humoresques, but as each of the pieces bears a descriptive title, Simrock snapped them up with glee together with the 'Love Songs'.

We do not know what the reason was for these months of creative inactivity. It is true that, at the time, his health was not of the best, but there was no reason for him to be depressed otherwise, and he no longer had those financial worries which had plagued his earlier years. The *Jacobín* had had its very successful première, his music was frequently performed in Prague and elsewhere, and he himself also conducted a concert of his own works in Dresden in March, including his Symphony No. 5 in F, which was very well received. In addition in January 1889 he was offered a post as Professor of Composition at the Prague Conservatorium – an offer which, after much deliberation, he declined in September as he felt that a teaching post would take up too much of the time which he needed for composing – and in May the Austrian Emperor awarded him the Order of the Iron Crown.

As usual, Dvořák betook himself to Vysoká in May 1889 to spend the summer there, and in July/August he composed his Piano Quartet in E flat (op.87), the first time that he had written for that combination since 1875. Unfortunately the work is overshadowed by the Piano Quintet in A of 1887 and has therefore tended to be treated as a sort of 'poor relation'. Granted, this E flat Quartet does not measure up to the standards which Dvořák had set in the Quintet, but it has the same mastery of integrating the piano with the string instruments to make it a true chamber work; it is formally compact and, if anything, it is melodically *too* rich in its inventiveness!

By now Dvořák was ready for another large-scale work, and only seven days after completing the piano quartet he started making thematic sketches for his next Symphony No. 8 in G. In the peace of Vysoká he then settled down on 6 September 1889 and completed the whole symphony in the form of a sketch by 23 September, and the full score by 8 November. The only event which interrupted this steady flow of composition was a short trip to Berlin in order to hear Hans von Bülow conduct the Symphony No. 7 in D minor on two successive days, 27 and 28 October – performances which impressed Dvořák so much that he subsequently pasted a photograph of von Bülow on the title page of the autograph score.

This G major Symphony (op.88) is certainly the most intimate and original within the whole canon of Dvořák's nine. It owes nothing to Brahms and does not share the dramatic drive and impact of its two predecessors. It treats the symphonic form much more loosely, but then this is exactly the treatment to which Dvořák had to subject his melodic material in order to achieve what he wanted to express. He himself has said that he wanted to write a work 'different from the other symphonies, with individual force worked out in a new way', and in this he certainly succeeded, even though perhaps in the Finale his Bohemian temperament got the better of him. It may lack some of those characteristics which we are accustomed to associate with the term 'symphony', and if it is surprising that people who love giving works descriptive tags have not called the Symphony No. 7 the 'Dramatic', it is equally surprising that the G major Symphony has never been subtitled the 'Idyllic'. The whole work breathes the spirit of Vysoká, and when one walks in those forests surrounding Dvořák's country home on a sunny summer's day, with the birds singing and the leaves of the trees rustling in a gentle breeze, one can virtually hear the music. Nor has the fact that the last movement is in a sort of free variation form instead of the classical mould of a symphonic Finale any bearing on the matter: this last movement just blossoms out, and I shall never forget Rafael Kubelik in a rehearsal, when it came to the opening trumpet fanfare, say to the orchestra; 'Gentlemen, in Bohemia the trumpets never call to battle – they always call to the dance!'.

The symphony has been praised and damned, and comments range from eulogistic praise (H. C. Colles: 'The Symphony in G, because of its freedom from precedent of any kind, may be said to be the crown of Dvořák's work') to downright condemnation (Gervase Hughes compares it to 'a meal of clear soup, a small slice of smoked salmon, a light egg soufflé and a water-ice'). Be that as it may; what is important is that it has remained a firm favourite with concert audiences the world over and among Dvořák's symphonies ranks second only in popularity to the 'New World'.

The work had its first performance in Prague on 2 February 1890 under Dvořák's direction, and then began the usual wrangling with Simrock who offered him a mere 1000 Marks with the familiar complaint that big works did not sell and that he would rather have short pieces. Dvořák, having received 6000 Marks from Simrock for his D minor Symphony, stood his ground and eventually, much to Simrock's disgust, sold it to Novello who published it in 1892 as No. 4 with a dedication to the Czech Academy of Science, Literature and the Arts to which Dvořák had been elected in April 1890. The fact that this is the only Dvořák symphony published by Novello has led to the unfortunate and inappropriate misnomer 'The English'. The relationship between Dvořák and Simrock at this point reached its lowest ebb.

1889 finished auspiciously, for in December Dvořák and his wife travelled to Vienna, where they were received in audience by Emperor Franz Josef who invested Dvořák with the Order of the Iron Crown, awarded in May. During the few days they spent in Vienna Dvořák met Brahms again. Then back to Prague, where Dvořák was visited by a deputation from Czech artistic circles congratulating him, and Christmas he spent as usual at home with his family.

1 January 1890 saw not only the beginning of a new decade, but also the beginning of a new major Dvořák work, for on that New Year's Day he started work on his *Requiem*. After the success of 'The Spectre's Bride' in Birmingham, he had been asked by R. H. Milward whether he would consider writing an oratorio for the 1888 Birmingham Festival, and Newman's *Dream of Gerontius* was suggested to him. Apparently Dvořák was sent a German translation of the text, but the

subject failed to appeal to him – which may be just as well, as it left the way clear for another composer much better qualified to set this particular text to music: Edward Elgar. However, Dvořák had not forgotten the request from Birmingham, even though 1888 was long past, and from the very beginning he had Birmingham in mind when writing the *Requiem*. It took him ten months to the day to complete it, for the final score was finished on 31 October 1890. How much this work meant to Dvořák, and how intensely he concentrated on it, is perhaps best evinced by the fact that no minor composition of any kind was allowed to intervene during this period. That is not to say that those ten months were devoid of excitement, for on the morning of 2 February he conducted the first performance of his G major Symphony in Prague, and this was followed up with a banquet in his honour in the evening of the same day. Towards the end of February he travelled to Russia with his wife where they spent the best part of the month of March.

The project of a visit to Russia had first been mooted when Tchaikovsky was in Prague in February 1888. At that time the two composers met quite frequently, for Tchaikovsky was present at a performance of Dvořák's Piano Quintet. They had lunch together at Dvořák's flat on the following day and dined at the Russian Circle on the next. When Tchaikovsky returned to Prague in November he could present Dvořák with an invitation from the Imperial Russian Music Society. After correspondence had gone to and fro and programmes had been discussed, Antonín and Anna set off for Moscow on 27 February 1890. To Dvořák's disappointment Tchaikovsky was in Italy at the time and could not welcome them, but he had taken all necessary steps to make sure that his friends were comfortable and well looked after. Dvořák's Moscow concert took place on 11 March, but the whole thing was somewhat unfortunate: the violinist who should have played Dvořák's Violin Concerto had fallen ill, and so the concert had to consist of works without a soloist. Russian audiences were not accustomed to this, nor were they used to programmes devoted to the works of a single composer. Dvořák conducted his Symphony in F, the *Adagio* from the Wind Serenade, the *Scherzo capriccioso*, the Slavonic Rhapsody No. 1, and the Symphonic Variations. The reception on the part of the audience was mixed – nothing like the tempestuous acclamation to which Dvořák had become accustomed during his English visits – but that was an experience to which Smetana had already been subjected several years earlier. The daily papers were even less complimentary and when, a few days later, the Dvořáks reached St. Petersburg (now Leningrad) Antonín wrote somewhat acidly to his friend Gustav Eim on 23 March:

> 'In the press these gentlemen didn't bother much about me – it was obvious that there were intrigues against me in the Russian music circles. Oh, thou so-called Slavonic brotherhood, where art thou?!'

In St. Petersburg, where he conducted the Symphony No. 6 and again the *Scherzo capriccioso*, the reception he received was much more heart-warming, and he must also have been buoyed by the fact that news reached him in Russia that the Czech University of Prague had nominated him a candidate for an Honorary Doctorate. At the little banquet given in his honour after the concert, Anton Rubinstein toasted him as 'our new Doctor of Music'.

From Russia Dvořák went straight to Olomouc to conduct his *Stabat Mater*, and by 26 March 1890 he was back in Prague, but not for long. He was made a Member of the Czech Academy of Sciences and Arts in April, and then he was off again to England for a brief stay in London to conduct the English première of the Symphony No. 8 on 24 April in St. James's Hall. The work received the ovations which Dvořák was used to in England and, though he only stayed for a few days, the time was long enough for him to have talks with Alfred Littleton (his father Henry having died in 1888) and sell the score to Novello as well as negotiate terms for the *Requiem* and the orchestration of the Mass in D. He returned to Prague before the end of the month, early in May he went to Vysoká for the summer, and now nothing was to interrupt work on the *Requiem* until it was finished. Four days after completing it he went to Frankfurt to conduct the *Husitská* Overture and the G major Symphony on 7 November 1890, and then back to Prague for the winter. Just before he left for Frankfurt the offer of a Professorship at the Prague Conservatorium was renewed, and this time Dvořák accepted.

His next trip took him to Olomouc in the company of his friends Bendl and Fibich to take part in the celebrations for the tenth anniversary of the Zerotín Choral Society, during the course of which he conducted his 149th Psalm. On his return to Prague on 17 November 1890 great news awaited him: the University of Cambridge had written, offering him an Honorary Doctorate. Was it this news that spurred Dvořák on to new compositions? No matter: the fact remains that shortly after his return to Prague he began to write what was to become one of his finest chamber music works – the Piano Trio (op.90) which is now known the world over as the *Dumky* Trio – 'Dumky' being the Czech plural for 'Dumka'. It is a completely original work which has no bearing on the classical concept of a piano trio, being a series of six movements, each in the style of a *Dumka*. They are thematically and tonally unrelated, and it is only because the first of them happens to be in the key of E minor that the work is very often wrongly referred to as the 'Piano Trio in E minor'. These *Dumkas* are in the simplest of forms, they are the uninhibited outpourings of a true Bohemian musician, and it is incomprehensible to me how anyone can fail to fall in love with this work. He completed the Trio by 12 February 1891, and Ferdinand Lachner, Hanuš Wihan and Dvořák himself gave the first performance in Prague on 11 April in a special concert to celebrate the fact that, on 17 March, Dvořák had had conferred on him by the Czech University the honorary degree of Doctor of Philosophy.

It was on 1 January 1891 that Dvořák officially became a Professor at the Prague Conservatorium, but it was not until the middle of January that he actually took up his teaching activities. Dvořák was at liberty to pick the most talented amongst the pupils, and in present-day language his composition class would be termed a Master Class. Among those whom he taught and who later made names for themselves as composers were Josef Suk (who also became his son-in-law), Oskar Nedbal, Vítězslav Novák and later – incredible though it may sound – Franz Lehár. By 13 May he had some of his pupils well enough groomed that he could present their works at a concert in the small hall of the Rudolfinum.

We now come to one of Dvořák's most important, most misunderstood and most underrated compositions – and I will call it one composition and not three: the Overtures now commonly known as 'In Nature's Realm' (*V Přírodě*, op.91), *Karneval* (op.92) and *Othello* (op.93), which he composed between March 1891 and January 1892. So far, in the orchestral field, Dvořák had abstained from writing the then fashionable type of programme music. Now, however, he had a new concept: he envisaged a cycle of three Concert Overtures (the way for which, as such, had already been paved by Beethoven, Weber, Mendelssohn and others) which he intended to call 'Nature, Life and Love'. Eventually he put this title aside and gave them the titles by which they are now known. It is a great pity that he did not keep to his original idea, thus making it perfectly clear that they are meant as a triptych, forcing conductors and promoters alike to adhere to his intentions, for these overtures are thematically so closely interrelated that they form an organic whole. In a way, they are a 'Symphony without a slow movement' just like Schumann's 'Overture, Scherzo and Finale' – and who would ever dream of performing those Schumann movements as separate items? They are the only overtures which Dvořák composed solely for performance in symphony concerts, completely divorced from any opera or stage production and, in this sense, they can be considered pointers towards those tone poems of 1896 which he wrote after his return from America. But it must be stressed that, whereas in the first two, 'In Nature's Realm' and *Karneval*, he still adheres to the formal principles which had guided him all his life, in *Othello* he makes a departure, just as he had done in his *Dumky* Trio. Instead of subjecting his inspiration to the dictates of a formal concept, he allows the music to be guided by the unfolding of the action of the play. In fact, he goes so far as to write various comments into his score to show precisely which point of the dramatic events the music is supposed to depict. Strangely enough, despite this unprecedented departure from his normal procedure, it is one of his finest overtures, though unfortunately also one of the most rarely performed, whereas *Karneval*, the weakest of the three, has become the most popular. Dvořák himself conducted the first performance of these overtures as a triptych in Prague on 28 April 1892 in his farewell concert before leaving for America and again, shortly after his arrival there, in New York on 21 October. However, in over thirty years of concert-going I can recall only one single instance that these three overtures have been played in the way in which they should be presented, namely as a whole, under the baton of Charles Groves. Otherwise, to get the true impression of the unity envisaged by Dvořák one has to resort to gramophone records. All three overtures were published by Simrock in 1894, and for once he gave the correct opus numbers.

To recapitulate: on 15 June 1891 Dvořák was due in Cambridge to conduct his Symphony in G, the *Stabat Mater*, and to collect his honorary Mus. D. A few days before his departure, the Dvořák household was aroused by a telegram from an American lady, Mrs. Jeanette Thurber. Mrs. Thurber, whose husband had become a millionaire as a wholesale grocer, was a woman of charm and of culture, and had an iron will as well as consummate competence in spending her husband's millions. Originally she had started an opera company in New York in competition to the 'Met' to provide opera sung in English, but this venture was discontinued when, after two years of existence, it had depleted the family bank account by a mere one and a half million dollars. Her next venture was to set up a National Conservatory of Music in New York, for which her first director was a Belgian singer, Jacques Bouhy. He ran the Conservatory very much along the lines of the Conservatoire National de Musique de Paris, where he had been a student, but he resigned in 1889 and returned to Europe. Let it be said to Mrs. Thurber's eternal credit that she did not just talk about philanthropy – she practised it! At her Conservatory pupils paid fees in accordance with what their parents could afford – if they could not afford tuition fees, their children were taught without paying anything at all – and there was no racial bar on Negroes or Red Indians: the only criterion was talent.

This telegram from Mrs. Thurber must really have shaken Dvořák, for no other Czech musician had ever before been offered that sort of post. He was to be Director of a Conservatory in New York; he was to work for eight months of the year, teaching three hours a day; he was to conduct a number of concerts annually of his own works – and he was to receive a yearly salary of $15,000 (in those days approximately the equivalent of 30,000 Gulden, whereas his annual salary at the Prague Conservatorium was 1200 Gulden), the contract to run for two years. For what seemed an eternity Dvořák wavered, discussed the matter with his friends, and corresponded with them about it. But Mrs. Thurber was a determined woman and, as usual, she got her own way. Eventually Dvořák, loath though he was to travel so far afield and leave his native Bohemia, accepted, having first assured himself that he would get leave from the Prague Conservatorium.

Dvořák was still busy composing the first of the three overtures, 'In Nature's Realm', when Mrs. Thurber's telegram arrived on 6 June 1891, and a few days later he set off for Cambridge. There he conducted the works he had promised to conduct, and the very next day, on 16 June, he was made an Honorary Doctor of Music of that University. He was greatly excited, but also slightly perturbed when he found that all the speeches were in Latin, of which he could not understand a word, nor could he reply in Latin. But no doubt Anna's presence was a staunch support, and he could also console himself with the fact that, in his own words, 'to compose the *Stabat Mater* was, after all, better than to know Latin'. While in Cambridge, Dvořák and his wife were the guests of Stanford. There are reports that Stanford was taken aback when he heard a noise in the garden in the early hours of the morning and saw the couple sitting under a tree at 6 a.m. So the English weren't early risers even in those days!

On his return to Prague he was present at a new production of his *Dimitrij*, conducted a performance of his own D major Symphony, and then he spent the rest of the summer in Vysoká, working on his cycle of overtures and only going up to Prague for the concert of compositions by his own pupils on 13 May. On 8 September 1891 there were also celebrations in Prague to mark his fiftieth birthday at which everyone of note was present – except Dvořák: he preferred to celebrate that day at Vysoká in the circle of his family.

Four days after his fiftieth birthday, on 12 September 1891, the *Karneval* Overture was finished, and shortly afterwards Dvořák had to pack his bags again to travel to Birmingham via London, his eighth trip to England in seven years and his last before his stay in America. He only remained long enough to rehearse and conduct the first performance of his *Requiem* at the Birmingham Music Festival, on 9 October, and Novello published the score in the same year. However, it must be stated that this publication does not incorporate certain last minute alterations which Dvořák had made, and in its authentic version the *Requiem* only appeared in 1961 in the Complete Edition of Dvořák's works, published by Artia, Prague. The *Requiem*, despite its warm reception at Birmingham, was not reviewed by the press as favourably as his earlier oratorios. Nevertheless, it stands head and shoulders above anything else that Dvořák wrote before or after in the liturgical field, including his later *Te Deum*, and is a work on the same elevated level as the Requiems by Mozart and Verdi. (In this context Brahms' *Ein deutsches Requiem* must be ignored, at it is not a Requiem in the liturgical sense of the word). This work has a thematic unity with that opening three-note motif on an upper and lower minor second gravitating round one central note which permeates the music from beginning to end and compulsively welds it into a whole, even though perhaps the average listener may only sense the effect without being able to pin-point the cause. In no other work that I can think of has Dvořák achieved such a concentrated unity, and I am at a loss to understand why this *Requiem* is heard so rarely, particularly in England for which it was written, and where choral music plays such an outstanding role. Surely we could have the occasional hearing of Dvořák's *Requiem* to replace just one or two performances of Handel's *Messiah*?!

From England Dvořák returned directly to Prague, arriving there no later than 12 October 1891, and towards the end of that month he signed a contract with Mrs. Thurber. Much wrangling had preceeded that momentous event. Dvořák had made his position quite clear, including the condition that he wanted half his salary deposited in Prague before he was prepared to sail – a very wise move, as subsequent events were to prove. Was this the guiding finger of his friend Rus (a judge), Littleton, or his wife Anna?

The eleven months which followed must have been among the most hectic in Dvořák's life. Naturally he had to fulfil his duties at the Prague Conservatorium, he himself wanted to complete the triptych of overtures – in fact, he began work on *Othello* in late November 1891 and finished it on 18 January 1892 – but he also prepared for what may be called a farewell tour of Bohemia prior to his departure for America. The cellist Hanuš Wihan must have been a particular friend of his, for Dvořák did something unprecedented: he sacrificed Christmas Day and Boxing Day 1891, days which were normally reserved exclusively for his family, to compose a Rondo in G minor (op.94) for Wihan to play on the extensive tour which they were about to undertake.

How Dvořák coped with everything during the first five

months of 1892 is hard to imagine. With his friend Ferdinand Lachner (violin), Hanuš Wihan, and himself as pianist, he toured the whole of Bohemia between 3 January and 29 May 1892. Each concert included the *Dumky* Trio, most of them the early Trio in G minor of 1876 as well, and Wihan gave the first performance of the Rondo in G minor on 6 January 1892 in Kladno. In the midst of all this Dvořák also conducted his *Requiem* in Olomouc and in Kroměříž, his early Symphony No. 4 in D minor in Prague, as well as the farewell concert in Prague mentioned earlier. In his spare moments he also managed to orchestrate his Mass in D for Novello. It is not unnatural that, in the midst of all these activities he could not find time to go to Vienna when the Prague National Theatre went there on tour in June 1892, even though his *Dimitrij* was being performed.

It has already been said that Mrs. Thurber was a determined woman. Having Dvořák's signed contract in her possession, she now began to badger him for a new composition, for it happened that Dvořák would be arriving in New York about a fortnight or so before the 400th anniversary of Columbus' arrival in the New World on 12 October 1492. Her suggestion was that he should set a poem, *The American Flag* by J. R. Drake, to music, and she would be sending him the text immediately. Dvořák agreed, but the text failed to arrive. When he had still not received it by June 1892, he decided to make the best use of the peace of Vysoká and composed his *Te Deum*. He considered – and quite rightly so – that a *Te Deum* might be a truly fitting work for such an occasion. When the text of *The American Flag* finally reached him, the time before his departure for America was running out and he could do no more than make a rough sketch of the piece.

INTERLUDIUM III::
LOCOMOTIVES AND PIGEONS

In the minds of the vast majority of people, the great musicians – whether they be composers or performers – exist in an idealized image, namely that which they present to the public. Few take the trouble to give a thought to the fact that these musicians are also ordinary human beings who live private lives and have their private interests and hobbies. Take Brahms, just as a case in point. That he was an avid reader on many subjects and an equally avid collector of musicians' autographs is not particularly surprising, for both somehow go hand in hand with his vocation as a composer. But for those who only know Brahms through the medium of his music and from photographs, it is an amazing revelation that this apparently severe and austere-looking composer with his awesome beard should also have been a fervent collector of toy soldiers, and apparently he not only collected them, but actually *played* with them in his leisure hours, few as they were. But this is a fact, and Brahms' hobby has been handed down to posterity, for his collection of toy soldiers is now housed in the *Kammerhofmuseum* in Gmunden, Upper Austria.

However, generally speaking the one hobby which seems to have fascinated a vast number of musicians is that of railways, locomotives, and trains. Some, myself and a few other musician friends of mine included, go in for miniature railways. The conductor Rudolf Kempe was one of these enthusiasts, and it is permissible to conjecture what might have thrilled him more: to acquire a new miniature locomotive, or to conduct a highly successful performance of Wagner's *Ring*. But the majority of musicians seem to have gone in for the real thing. Apart from minor compositions, Honegger was perhaps the first composer to express his great love for locomotives in music, in his *Mouvement Symphonique 'Pacific 231'* of 1923, and he himself said about it: 'I have always had a passion for locomotives. To me they are living beings, whom I love as others love women or horses.' At the time of its first performance the novelty of the work must have shattered the audience – which will not have been the case with Villa-Lobos' *Bachianas Brasileiras No. 2* subtitled 'The Little Train of the Caipira', an endearing and charming piece for chamber orchestra written in 1931 which has become a firm concert favourite. Eugène Goossens, conductor and composer, never wrote any 'railway music', but he also was fanatical about locomotives and liked to drive a real engine whenever this could be arranged. There was a famous occasion when he took the Sydney Symphony Orchestra on a country tour to Newcastle, N.S.W., and when the train arrived there the players found to their amazement that the 'boss' lumbered from the engine – he had driven them there himself. After an exhilarating concert the Newcastle press reported the following day: GOOSSENS DRIVES TO AND IN NEWCASTLE.

Perhaps Dvořák was the first locomotive enthusiast among all the musicians attracted to this particular hobby. In 1850, when he was nine years old, the railway line from Prague to Kralupy – which passed through Nelahozeves – was opened, and this was the first time that 'Toník' saw a railway train. It has been suggested that it was this experience which stimulated his great love; alternatively it is also possible that his stay with Aunt Josefa in Prague (whose husband Václav Dušek was a railway employee) may have influenced him in that direction. It is certainly true that both from Aunt Josefa's home in the Karlovo Náměsti as well as from his flat in Žitná, it was only a relatively short walk to Prague's main railway station. As far as I can discover, Dvořák never actually drove a locomotive himself, nor does he seem to have had any ambitions in that direction, but we do know that in a very short time he had struck up a friendship with station masters, engine drivers, stokers and the like and knew precisely which locomotive under whose guidance was taking out what train and to where. It was a matter of great annoyance to him when his professional duties prevented him from going in person to the railway station to witness the departure of some express train. Alec Robertson tells a delightful story of how, one day when he himself was prevented from going, he sent his pupil Josef Suk to go and find out the number of the locomotive which was taking out the express that day. Suk, who at that time was already courting Dvořák's daughter Otilie, came back with the number, not of the engine but of the coal-tender – and Dvořák angrily confronted Otilie with the words: 'So that's the kind of man you want to marry!' Of course, music was the ruling passion of his life, yet in later years he once said to his students at the Prague Conservatorium – these words are perpetuated on the walls of the Dvořák Museum at the Country Estate of Count Kaunic in Vysoká: 'I would gladly give all my symphonies, had I been able to invent the locomotive!'*

In addition to this Dvořák was a great nature-lover. He was an early riser, and first thing in the morning he enjoyed going for a walk among the trees. In Prague this hobby had to be restricted to the Karlovo Náměsti, but once he had his country house in Vysoká he could really roam the forests. He adored all birds, and particularly pigeons. Once he had settled in Vysoká he could really concentrate on his hobby. It started with merely keeping pigeons, but rapidly developed into pigeon breeding. We have pictures of Dvořák sitting on the bench at Vysoká, surrounded by his feathered friends, and he must, in the course of time, have become quite an expert, as is

*Všechny své symfonie bych dal za to, kdybych byl vynašel lokomotivu.

shown in a letter which he wrote to the choir master Strniště in Moravia. This musician was also a great lover of pigeons and made Dvořák a present of some rare specimens. Dvořák thanked him as follows:

'. . . My reason for not writing [earlier] was that I wanted to know whether these beautiful pigeons would settle. I waited long till at last my efforts were rewarded. The French ones took their time about it – they showed no inclination to go into the dovecot with the other pigeons and only yesterday we put the "black tiger" with the black pigeon, so that I think everything is all right and there will be no more trouble.

It was really comical, I can tell you. The whole day I was running from one cottage to another in the village for fear the "Frenchies" might fly away. Everybody who passes by stops to look at the lovely creatures. All the pigeon-fanciers here are talking about them. . . .'

But apart from pigeons he loved all birds and, under the eaves of his house in Vysoká, he had numerous small cages full of the little songsters. It is easy to understand his enthusiasm, but whether or not it was particularly kind to these little denizens of the open air and sky to be so tightly pent up is a matter of personal opinion. We must not forget, however, that the approach to such matters in the late 1890s was somewhat different from our present-day attitude.

During his years in America, Dvořák was put to a severe strain where his hobbies were concerned. There was little chance of 'locomotive spotting' in New York, and pigeons could only be seen in the aviary in Central Park, so for a while he transferred some of his enthusiasm to ships. A quotation is interesting here from the reminiscences of J. J. Kovařík who, after all, was with Dvořák during the whole of his American period and therefore speaks from first-hand experience:

'What the Master missed in America were his pigeons and locomotives. He felt the want of these two "hobbies" very much, but here, too, he at length found a modest substitute. One day we went with the Master* to the Central Park where there is a small Zoological Garden and buildings with different kinds of birds. And then we came to a huge aviary with about two hundred pigeons. It was a real surprise for the Master and his pleasure at seeing the pigeons was great, and even though none of these pigeons could compare with his "pouters" and "fantails", we made the trip to Central Park at least once and often twice a week.

With locomotives it was a more difficult matter. In New York at that time, there was only one station – the others were across the river. . . . At the main station they did not allow anybody on to the platform except the passengers and it was in vain that we begged the porter to let us look at the "American locomotive". We travelled by overhead tram to 155th Street, a good hour from the Master's house, and there, on a bank, waited for the Chicago or Boston express to go by. Only it took up a lot of time, nearly the whole afternoon, as we always waited for a number of trains so that it would be worth the journey – and then the Master found a new hobby in steamships. For one thing the harbour was much nearer and then, on the day of departure, the public was allowed on board, an opportunity which the Master made full use of.

There was soon not a boat that we had not inspected from stem to stern. The Master always started a conversation with the ship's captain or with his assistants, and so, in a short time, we knew all the captains and mates by name. And when a ship was due to sail we went there and watched it from the shore till it was out of sight. If it happened that the Master remained a little longer than usual at the Conservatory or was

---

*In the English text of Kovařik's reminiscences from which I am quoting, he always refers to Dvořák as the 'Master', presumably as a sort of parallel to 'Maestro', 'Maître', 'Meister'. For want of a better English word I have let 'Master' stand.

engrossed in his work at home and so forgot about the
departure of the boat and there was no longer time to go
to the harbour, we went by overhead tram to Battery
Park . . . and from there followed the ship in her outward
journey for as long as she remained in sight.'

One other pastime must be mentioned which has nothing to
do with locomotives and pigeons. During the later years of his
life he took to gymnastics and skittles. The latter was mainly
prompted by his association in the local inns of the nearest
major town to Vysoká, Příbram, with the working class
population of this coal-mining area. In his memoirs his son
Otakar writes as follows:

'Something that is perhaps quite unknown to the general
public is that Father was very keen on gymnastics which
at first consisted in taking a chair and doing arm exercises
with it. Later he got himself dumb-bells and exercised
with them early in the morning. He was also something of
a sportsman. His sport was skittles at Vysoká. Almost
every Sunday forenoon, and usually Thursday afternoon
as well, was devoted to a game of skittles, in an alley
situated at the foot of the garden. The set of skittles is still
kept at Vysoká as a much-prized souvenir.'

As we are considering the composer Antonín Dvořák, all these
little details could appear insignificant, trivial, and irrelevant,
but in fact they are not: they enable us to reconstruct in our
minds the personality of a man who was simple, kindly, and
who loved nature. It is this simplicity, in conjunction with his
fervent nationalism, which provides us with a key to his music.

THE AMERICAN PERIOD

Dvořák left Vysoká on 10 September 1892, probably with tears in his eyes, and after spending a few days in Prague he went to Bremen with his wife and his children Otilie and Antonín, leaving the remaining four children for the time being in the care of their maternal grandmother. On 17 September the four Dvořáks embarked on the *S.S. Saale* bound for New York, the party also comprising a fifth member: Josef Jan Kovařík (1870-1951). Kovařík's parents were Czechs who had emigrated to Spillville, Iowa, in the middle of the 19th century, and Kovařík was born there. He had then come to Bohemia to study the violin at the Prague Conservatorium and, having finished his studies, was about to go back home. Dvořák had met him at the Conservatorium, and when he found out that the young man was about to return to his native America he quickly seized the opportunity and engaged him as a guide-*cum*-secretary. In a way Kovařík is of great importance to us, because for three years he formed an integral part of the Dvořák household, and therefore his 'Reminiscences' were based on a close personal contact with all persons and events concerned. Granted, at times he got some minor details wrong, but this is a small matter compared to the vital authenticity he supplies and the feel of events which took place almost a century ago. Here is his own description of how he came to join Dvořák:

' ... When, on taking my final examinations at the Conservatoire, I mentioned that I would be leaving as soon as possible for America, the Master said quite simply: "You know what – we shall do it like this: you will wait until September and then we shall go nicely together." On my asking what I should do in Bohemia for two whole months, the Master said: "You will come for the holidays to our place at Vysoká and then we shall set out together for America!" And that was what happened.'

The whole of the crossing, during which the *Saale* put in briefly at Southampton, took nine days, and in the Atlantic they ran into a storm. All the passengers kept to their cabins, and it is amusing that Dvořák, who once had dreaded the channel crossing, was the only one who did not become seasick: he alone had the stomach to go down to the dining room at meal times and share a table with the ship's captain. Perhaps it was during those conversations over their after-dinner cigars that Dvořák's later interest in the matter of ocean-going liners was first stimulated.

The *Saale* reached Staten Island on 26 September 1892, but because of an outbreak of cholera somewhere in Europe she was kept there in quarantine for 24 hours. (In those days, Ellis Island had no great significance, even though half a century or so later notable musicians such as De Sabata and Josef Krips had to spend a short involuntary holiday there because they had given concerts in the Soviet Union!)

In any event, the Dvořáks set foot on *terra firma* in New York on 27 September 1892 and were greeted enthusiastically by the Secretary of the National Conservatory and a whole contingent from the New York Czech community. Their first abode was the Clarendon Hotel on the corner of Fourth Avenue and East 18th Street, but hotel life never suited Dvořák very well – and this one was noisy and expensive – and soon the family moved into a house at 327 East 17th Street, only two blocks away from the National Conservatory where he had to attend to his duties. For one thing Dvořák preferred a home, for another it was much cheaper, and also the firm of Steinway provided him, without charge, with a grand piano – as he wrote to his friends, the Hlávkas, in Prague: '. . . so that we have one nice piece of furniture in our sitting-room'. 327 East 17th Street remained his New York base for the whole of his stay in America.

Dvořák's first weeks in New York were very lively. There were invitations and receptions: on 1 October 1892 Mrs. Thurber introduced him to the members of her National Conservatory, and on 9 October there was a concert and banquet in his honour given by the New York Czech community – just the sort of thing which Dvořák disliked intensely. At this juncture it is perhaps worth mentioning something about the American Czechs. It has often been said that there are more Irishmen in the New York Police Force than in the whole of Ireland. It is perhaps reasonable to assume that in the 1890s a certain parallel could be drawn: there were probably more expatriate Czechs living in America than in Bohemia. New York boasted a large Czech population, so did other big cities such as Omaha, Chicago and St. Paul, and as far as smaller centres are concerned, more will be said about that when we come to talk about Spillville. Needless to say, wherever he went these Czech communities knew of Dvořák's music, looked on him as a national hero, and acclaimed and fêted him wildly.

Dvořák's first appearance as a conductor took place at Carnegie Hall in the famous concert for Columbus' 400th anniversary on 21 October. It was to have taken place on 12 October, but for some reason had to be postponed and, after all, after 400 years do nine days really make much difference? The concert opened with *My Country 'tis of thee*, then followed a speech, and Seidl conducted Liszt's *Tasso*. After that it was Dvořák's turn. First he conducted his three Overtures 'In Nature's Realm', *Karneval* and *Othello* played as a cycle, probably the first performance in this presentation in America, and finally came the première of the *Te Deum*. Much criticism had been levelled against this work – that it is extrovert, brash, noisy. It is true that, musically speaking, it can in no way bear comparison with the *Requiem*, and Dvořák makes lavish use of trumpet fanfares and timpani; but then there is a subtle difference between a Requiem and a Te Deum. Dvořák gives us the full impact of his personal praise to the Lord, so let the philistines pick out the musical faults under their magnifying glasses: given a good performance, it is a stirring and rousing hymn to the Glory of God, and it brought his New York audience out of their seats cheering with enthusiasm.

We have seen earlier how Dvořák had wavered when it came to signing a contract with Mrs. Thurber. Now that he was in New York, he was in two minds as to whether he liked America or not. He certainly did not like New York as a city: for him, the 'simple Bohemian musician', the town was too big, too bustling, too blustering. His haven was the *Café Fleishman* on the corner of Broadway and 10th Street, where he was a regular visitor, just as he was in Prague in the *Pařížska Kavárna* (the 'Paris café').* That his hobbies – locomotives and pigeons – suffered sorely we have already seen, and in any case Mrs. Thurber had little understanding for such vagaries on the part of the Director of her Conservatory. However, as a woman she appears to have had some sympathy for his great interest in the Europe-bound liners and the nostalgia for his homeland connected with these ships.

On the other hand, what held a tremendous appeal for Dvořák was democracy, the freedom of America, and the equality of human beings. He wrote to Josef Michl:

'. . . Here the millionaire comes to his servant and says:

---

*The Clarendon Hotel and the *Café Fleishman*, true to American tradition, have long since been knocked down. By some miracle, 327 East 17th Street survived and, in 1954 on the 50th anniversary of Dvořák's death, a memorial plaque was unveiled there. The coffee house opposite the Žitná 14 (present-day numbering) still stands, though under a different name, and should you ever find yourself in Prague any waiter there will gladly show you that corner table which was, so to speak, Dvořák's private domain.

"Sir!" – and the servant, although he knows that he is speaking to a millionaire, also calls him "Sir!". They are each other's equals – apart from the millions of dollars . . .'

Of course this is more than a slight exaggeration, but that is how it struck Dvořák at the time. He was equally impressed when he went to Boston in November 1892 to conduct his *Requiem*: ticket prices for the performance on 30 November were astronomical and only within the reach of the very well-off, but on the day before there was what might be called a 'public rehearsal' at ludicrously low admission prices for the working population who were earning a minimal wage, so that they also should have a chance of hearing the music, and for a financial outlay which they could afford.

During his first months in America Dvořák conducted his Symphony No. 6 in D on 17 November in New York and the performance of the *Requiem* just mentioned in Boston, but apart from that his life was fairly monotonous. Three days a week he held his composition classes at the Conservatory, and twice a week he conducted the Conservatory Orchestra. He knew no distinction of nationality, race, or religion; for him there existed only one difference: that between good and bad music, and in this attitude he was whole-heartedly supported by Mrs. Thurber. As time went on, he interested himself keenly in the music of Negroes and Red Indians as well as their folklore. Mrs. Thurber suggested to him that he should write an opera on the subject of the *Hiawatha* Legend, and for quite a time he toyed with the idea, even making some sketches for it. But in the end no suitable libretto could be found and the whole project was discarded.

Dvořák's first academic year in America, apart from the trip to Boston, was spent in New York. In those days, New York could boast the Metropolitan Opera House, the New York Philharmonic (conducted by Anton Seidl) and the Symphony Society (conducted by Walter Damrosch). The Boston Symphony Orchestra then had Artur Nikisch as its principal conductor. Visiting artists from Europe were the order of the day but, seen as a whole, Dvořák went to few concerts or operatic performances. In Bohemia his motto had been 'early to bed, early to rise', and he stuck to these principles in America, where musical performances tended to start late. As far as we can gather from various reports, he only went to the 'Met' twice and did not even bother to attend performances of his own works if it did not suit him. However, he frequently met his friends at the *Café Fleishman*, among them the conductor Anton Seidl, with whom he was in complete agreement on musical matters, although he found it difficult to reconcile Seidl's agnostic, not to say atheistic views with his own firm faith.

During the first year of his American 'stint' he performed a task as a matter of duty: he set J. R. Drake's poem *The American Flag* to music. It was first performed in New York on 4 May 1895 after Dvořák had left the continent for good. Even Šourek and Clapham, those most ardent admirers of Dvořák, find it difficult to give this work any word of commendation; Dvořák was never very good at writing patriotic works to order, and its best moment is probably when an *alla marcia* bursts into a Polka, a far cry from the Stars and Stripes. As far as I know this is one of the very few of original compositions which Dvořák himself never heard, nor did he insist upon a performance!

During the first half of 1893 he made one appearance only as a conductor in New York. R. H. Warren had programmed a performance of 'The Spectre's Bride' and invited Dvořák to conduct his Overture *Husitská* as a curtain raiser – presumably as an audience attraction as well. In April he also received the news that he had been elected a Regular Member of the Berlin Academy of Fine Arts – the greatest honour, with the exception of the Cambridge Doctorate, to be awarded to Dvořák from outside the Austro-Hungarian Empire. Apart from his activities as director and teacher of the Conservatory he could please himself and so, having safely got *The American Flag* out of the way, he now settled down to

.compose something he really wanted to write. It was none other than his Symphony No. 9 in E minor, 'From the New World' (*Z nového světa*, op.95) which he began on 10 January and completed on 24 May 1893.

The 'New World' Symphony poses a problem. There is no denying that it is Dvořák's most popular work, and a very great one. But it must also be admitted, as many critics have pointed out, that it is weak on formal grounds. In his early symphonies one can accuse Dvořák of being guilty of over-inventiveness and consequent lack of form. By now he had the mastery to keep a firm grip on his material, so there is none of this diffuseness which mars his early symphonic works. But there is still an *embarras de richesse* in his melodic outpourings, and despite his extremely craftsman-like way of creating unity, in each movement, by bringing reminiscences and echoes of what has gone before, almost in the manner of the so-called 'cyclic' principle, the strict form becomes somewhat blurred, particularly in the Finale. One can, of course, cite the example of the preceding Symphony No. 8 which, likewise, does not pattern itself on a stereotyped symphonic concept, but here he acted the way he did for essentially different reasons. Nevertheless the Symphony No. 9 is of tremendous proportions and its major drawback is that it is played too frequently – and often inadequately in run-of-the-mill performances.

But the other problem is the alleged use of Negro melodies, and this also applies to the chamber music which he composed a few weeks later during his holiday in Spillville. It is true that Dvořák had the greatest love and respect for these tunes, as he once said in an interview with a journalist of the *New York Herald*:

'. . . In the negro melodies of America I discover all that is needed for a great and noble school of music. They are pathetic, tender, passionate, melancholy, solemn, religious, bold, merry, gay or what you will . . . There is nothing in the whole range of composition that cannot be supplied with themes from this source.'

It is also true that some of his melodies bear a distinct resemblance to *Deep River* and *Swing Low, Sweet Chariot*. But too much nonsense has been talked and written about this 'American' aspect. To start off with, Dvořák never used any original Negro melodies in his compositions, and he cannot be blamed if later his themes have been furnished with texts as Negro Spirituals. He stressed again and again that, whereas the symphony was obviously written under the influence of his early American impressions, there was no intention of reproducing folk songs. For let us not forget that the pentatonic scale is not the private property of any one nation: with our greatly increased knowledge of the music of the Orient we now realize that it is the common possession of the Far East and of India, stretching all the way across the Middle East and Europe to the Americas. So the mere fact that a melody is pentatonic is no evidence as to whether that melody is American or Slavonic. When writing to the Czech conductor Oskar Nedbal in 1900 he said quite definitely: '. . . but the nonsense – that I made use of "Indian" and American motives – leave out, because it is a lie . . .' and he is also reported as having said: 'Whatever I have written in America, England or elsewhere is and always remains Bohemian music.' However, perhaps the most important evidence once again comes from the reminiscences of Kovařík:

'One day at the café, Seidl said that he had heard that the Master has a *new symphony* and asked him for permission to perform it at one of the next concerts of the New York Philharmonic. The Master thought it over – but on taking leave he promised to give Seidl the Symphony to perform. That was in the middle of November 1893. The following day Seidl informed the Master that the symphony would be given at the concert to be held about 15th December and that he should send him the score as soon as possible. The same evening, before I set out with the score, the Master wrote at the last minute on the titlepage, *Z nového světa* ("From the New World"). Till then there was [*sic*] only E minor Symphony No. 8. The title "From the New World" caused then and still causes today, at least here in America, much confusion and division of opinion. There were and are many people who thought and think that the title is to be understood as meaning the "American" symphony, i.e. a symphony with American music. Quite a wrong idea! This title means nothing more than "Impressions and Greetings from the New World" – as the Master himself more than once explained. And so when at length it was performed and when the Master read all sorts of views on it whether he had or had not created an "American" music, he smiled and said, "It seems that I have got them all confused" and added: "At home they will understand at once what I meant."

In the early part of that year 1893, while at work on the 'New World' Symphony, Dvořák came to a great decision. It had been his intention to return to Bohemia for the summer vacation, and when the train pulled out of Prague station on the first lap of his journey to America in the previous September, his last words of farewell to his friends were: 'See you in the summer'. Now, however, after hearing all about Spillville from Kovařík he changed his mind, and perhaps he was also influenced by the thought that, having once travelled all the way to America, he might as well see something more of the country, meet other Czech communities, and at the same time visit the Chicago World Exhibition. But he could not bear the thought of being separated from his other four children any longer, and so he had them brought over to America by another sister of his wife's, Mrs. Terezie Koutecká, accompanied by a nanny. Mrs. Koutecká and her charges departed from Bohemia on 21 May 1893, reaching Southampton on 24

May – from where Dvořák received a cable from them on the very day that he wrote *Finis* on the score of the 'New World' Symphony – and on 31 May the party landed in New York. Needless to say, Dvořák was overjoyed at having all his loved ones with him again.

There must have been an enormous hustle and bustle in the Dvořák household during the next three days, for 3 June was the date set for the departure to Spillville in the Middle West. The faithful Kovařík once again took over all the travel arrangements, which cannot have been easy, for they involved conveying no less than eleven people from New York to Spillville, Iowa, a matter of about 1300 miles: Dvořák and his wife with her sister, the six children, the nanny and, of course, Kovařík himself. They started off at eight on a Saturday morning and finally reached their destination at lunchtime on 5 June. Of course the journey went in stages: from New York they took the Chicago Express, then a few hours in Chicago, and after that two more trains of diminishing proportions which finally landed them at Calmar, still ten miles or so from Spillville. Whether Dvořák ever got any sleep on this trip is doubtful, for whenever there was a stop where they had to change locomotives he was out of his berth, busy looking at the engines, taking down their numbers and (probably) talking to the drivers. If in those days tourists had carried cameras as they do now, I am sure he would have used up rolls and rolls of film. But quite apart from locomotives he must also have enjoyed the ever-varying countryside on this, his longest journey apart from Atlantic crossings.

The whole organization for their arrival and stay in Spillville, Josef Kovařík had delegated to his parents. Together with the local priest they met the whole crowd at Calmar station and provided pony traps to get the party from there to Spillville, where Kovařík's father had found them a house which could accommodate them all. Although it was a square, box-like affair Dvořák fortunately approved. But it was not only the house but Spillville itself which met with Dvořák's whole-hearted approval, for it really was a sort of Bohemia transplanted to America.* Granted, there was no railway station for him to study the locomotives, the little river Turkey was too small to carry large boats, and although there were birds in plenty there were no pigeons. But on the other hand, Spillville lay in a rolling, hilly countryside which reminded him of Vysoká and Nelahosevez, he could stop and talk to anyone in the street in Czech, and even the local butcher was called Dvořák! In those days the population of Spillville numbered about 300 – according to a talk given on the BBC in 1978 by Anthony King, who has visited Spillville on more than one occasion, this has now risen to 361. The months spent in Spillville were the happiest in the whole of Dvořák's American period. He followed the usual routine of his days at Vysoká: he rose early, went for a walk, and then attended early Mass. He did so on the very day after his arrival, and when he came to the church (which, needless to say, was called St. Wenceslas) he immediately made his way to the organ, without asking for permission. How great was the surprise of the congregation when suddenly they heard that old Czech hymn *Bože před tvou velebností* ('O God before Thy Majesty'), and from that moment onward they knew that he was 'one of them'. Every morning for the rest of his stay in Spillville he either played the organ or led the choir in church, and at times his wife joined him on Sundays with her beautiful contralto voice.

As there were no 'hobbies' to pursue, Dvořák again settled down to composition. Within the incredibly short period of three days, between 8 and 10 June 1893, he sketched out his String Quartet No. 12 in F major (op.96), and by 23 June the score was completed. Dvořák was very happy about the work, for at the end of the sketch he wrote: 'Thanks be to God, I am satisfied, it went quickly.' He was so eager to hear it that he

---

*In those days the Catholic priest of Spillville was Tomáš Bílý. The house where Dvořák lived is still standing. There were later two brothers Bílý (whether related to the priest I do not know) who were passionately interested in clocks. The house is now known as the *Bílý Clock Museum*, but a room is also devoted to the memory of Dvořák and contains among other exhibits the organ – or more correctly harmonium – which Dvořák regularly played during his stay in Spillville.

immediately commandeered three other players besides himself – namely three members of the Kovařík family – to give it a rough play-through (the term 'rough' probably being the operative word) and it can safely be said that this F major Quartet has since become the most popular of all his string quartets. Only three days after completing it, Dvořák began to compose another chamber music work, a String Quintet in E flat (op.97) for two violins, two violas and cello, by far the greater work of the two, and he finished the score on 1 August 1893.

Much of what has been said about the 'New World' Symphony also applies to these two works: they are and always will remain pure Dvořák, pure Bohemian music, despite claims to the contrary. It is true that Dvořák thought highly of the Negro songs, and that at the time when he was finishing the F major Quartet he heard Red Indians singing and making music in Spillville – in fact, he got Kovařík to note down a melodic fragment which he later utilised in the E flat Quintet. But in the crucible of Dvořák's musical invention this fragment is transformed: it is no longer recognizable as being 'Red Indian' and becomes just plain Bohemian Dvořák, as do the reminiscences of Negro tunes in the 'New World' Symphony and the String Quartet – nowadays known as the 'American'. When speaking about this quartet in a BBC broadcast, Richard Graves very aptly referred to it as 'eating Blueberry Pie and washing it down with Slivovic', and in an article in *Czech Music*, the Journal of the Dvořák Society (Vol. 8, No. 1, London, January 1982) William Alwyn writes with great perspicacity:

'. . . then there is the vitality and freshness of the Czech folk idiom which permeates all Dvořák's finest music – even the tunes in *From the New World* seem more Czech than negro in origin when transmuted into Dvořák's unmistakeable idiom and harmonization. This is also true of the lovely F major String Quartet – once affectionately known as the "Nigger" Quartet and now through absurd racial prejudice labelled inappropriately the "American" Quartet! – and his vivid use of orchestral colour. . . .'

Everything has already been told about the quarrels between Dvořák and Simrock over the publication of Symphony No. 8 and the *Requiem*, the long break in communication between the two men and how, during Dvořák's holiday, they reached agreement by letter. Dvořák duly sent off a parcel containing the scores of the *Dumky* Trio, the three Overtures, the 'New World' Symphony, the String Quartet in F plus some minor works from Spillville, and they actually reached Simrock in Berlin – postal services must have been better in those days than they are now. Simrock immediately had the works engraved, and then a minor miracle happened: in order to save the delay of sending the proofs back and forth across the Atlantic to be corrected, he asked Brahms whether he would read the proofs. Brahms did so, and anyone who has every had the laborious job of proof-reading music manuscripts will echo me in saying that 'greater love hath no man than he who reads another composer's proofs' – a sure token of the high esteem in which Brahms held Dvořák, and of the friendship between these two great musicians.

During the holiday in Spillville Dvořák undertook two trips. The first was a matter of a week or so in Chicago, where the World Fair was being held. He took his two eldest children on this journey, the daughters Otilie and Anna, for there was a special Czech day (12 August 1893) with a concert of Czech music. On that occasion Dvořák conducted his G major Symphony and some Slavonic Dances, as well as the overture 'My Home'. The second excursion he made with his wife and Kovařík between 1 and 5 September. In Omaha and St. Paul he visited acquaintances and, of course, wherever he went he was fêted by the Czech communities, as he had also been in Chicago. While in St. Paul he took a little tour to the Minnehaha Falls which impressed him very much, and on his starched shirt cuff he jotted down a short theme which later was to become the basis of the slow movement of his Sonatina for violin and piano.

The remaining ten days were spent in Spillville, and then duty called him back to New York. This time the whole Dvořák family took the long way round. First going back to Chicago, they then cut through Canada to see the Niagara Falls, and at this gigantic spectacle of nature Dvořák reputedly exclaimed: 'By God, that'll be a Symphony in B minor!' This has been interpreted by many people as being a pointer towards the Cello Concerto, but let it not be forgotten that the very first sketch of that Cello Concerto was conceived in D minor (See illustration 55).

By 21 September 1893 Dvořák was back in New York and back in harness. The months that followed must have been months of hard work, but also months of discontent for, after that happy summer in Spillville, he found it difficult to settle down again to the life of New York which, in any case, he had never particularly liked. This may account for the fact that during the first nine weeks after his return he started sketching out quite a few works and then discarded them, and the only positive results were the orchestral versions of two pieces for cello and piano: the Rondo in G minor and *Klid* ('Silent Woods') (op.94 and op. 68/5 resp.). He also arranged Stephen Foster's *Old Folks at Home* for soli, chorus and orchestra, but the only work of importance which he composed during these last three months of 1893 was the Sonatina in G for violin and piano. He had recently tried to bring some sort of order into the opus numbers of his works, and he fondly believed this to be his op.100, so he wanted it to have some special significance. It has been stressed more than once how much his family meant to Dvořák, and he decided to write a Sonatina which would – in theory – be within the technical reach of children. He dedicated it to all his children, although the original dedication was only to Otilie and Antonín, the other four names being added later. It is a charming little work, incorporating the melody which he had scribbled on his shirt cuff at the Minnehaha Falls, and he was fully justified in telling Simrock that, though written for youngsters, many a grown-up would enjoy playing it as well. Like other composers – take Mozart's C major Piano Sonata K.545 entitled 'A Little Piano Sonata for Beginners' – he wrote what is seemingly a simple piece, but it takes true mastery to play it.

Despite his despondency, the year 1893 was to end in a burst of glory, for on 16 December Anton Seidl conducted the first performance of the 'New World' Symphony in New York's Carnegie Hall. It is always easy for a composer to over-estimate the success of a work at its première, but that was not the case on this occasion, and Dvořák was fully justified in writing to Simrock:

> '. . . The success of the symphony was tremendous; the papers write that no composer has ever had such success. I was in a box; the hall was filled with the best New York audience, the people clapped so much that I had to thank them from the box like a king!? *alla* Mascagni in Vienna (don't laugh!) . . .'

There is no need to tell anyone that this initial success was no mere flash in the pan, for the 'New World' has ever since remained one of the handful of symphonies which are firm favourites the world over.

How Dvořák spent Christmas 1893 we do not know, but it surely must have been a happy one for him as he was surrounded by the whole of his family, and on the very first day of the New Year 1894 the Kneisel Quartet gave the first performance of the String Quartet in F in Boston. Dvořák himself could not be present, but they repeated it on 12 January in Carnegie Hall, also including the first performance of the String Quintet in E flat in their programme as well as the A major Sextet which Joachim had popularized so much on his tours.

The rest of this first stay in America until the whole family returned to Bohemia in May was not particularly happy for

Dvořák. Work at the Conservatory continued as before, and he also conducted a concert of the Conservatory Orchestra in which negroes participated and at which he gave the first performance of his arrangement *Old Folks at Home*. But the relationship with Mrs. Thurber became more and more strained as she fell into arrears with the payment of Dvořák's salary, and it was only after obtaining definite and binding promises from her regarding settlement of the monies due to him that Dvořák signed another contract to return for a six month period from November 1894 to April 1895. Under the circumstances it is not surprising that compositions did not flow so freely from his pen. In February/March he composed a little Suite in A for piano (op.98) which in January 1895 he orchestrated (op.98b). It is for some reason customary to denigrate this Suite, but I fail to see why. Granted, it is not a work of major significance, but it is full of charm and makes most attractive listening in both its forms, though Dvořák himself never heard the orchestral version.

On the personal front he received nothing but bad tidings. During that winter 1893/94 two musicians who were close personal friends died: Tchaikovsky and Hans von Bülow. On top of it he received news of his father's illness, and shortly afterwards he died in Velvary in his eightieth year. It may easily have been these sad events which inspired him to write the ten Biblical Songs (*Biblické Písné*, op.99) for voice and piano in March 1894. They were to be the last songs he composed and are beyond doubt his greatest. For the texts he drew on an old Czech translation of the Book of Psalms. Apparently already at the time of writing these he had the idea at the back of his mind to orchestrate them, and eventually he did so in January 1895 at about the same time when he also orchestrated the Piano Suite in A. For some reason for which no-one seems to have an explanation he orchestrated only the first five, and the remaining Nos. 6-10 were later orchestrated by the Czech conductor Vilém Zemánek. (These last five songs have since been scored again by Jarmil Burghauser and Jan Hanuš.) It is also of interest that Dvořák conducted the first performance of the five songs at the Rudolfinum in Prague on 4 January 1896, that memorable occasion when the Czech Philharmonic Orchestra as such made its first public appearance.* In passing, it is perhaps also worth noting that the third of these Biblical Songs has distinct reminiscences of Wagner's *Tristan*.

There is little else to tell of the remaining months of Dvořák's first stay in America. He did his work at the Conservatory and devoted the rest of his time to revising *Dimitrij*, a revision which he finally completed in Vysoká in the summer of 1894. But there was one little 'happening' which, at the time, may have seemed completely unimportant and yet was to have a far-reaching effect. On 5 April 1894 he attended a concert in Brooklyn at which his Symphony No. 9 was being performed. The programme also included the first performance of the Cello Concerto in E minor, op.30, by Victor Herbert, the then principal cellist of the New York Philharmonic Orchestra. Needless to say, Victor Herbert himself was the soloist, though later he was to become far more famous as a composer of operettas and musicals. Now Dvořák had never really considered the cello as a solo instrument – in his own words, 'it twangs at the top and mumbles at the bottom'. Whether it was at the insistence of his friend Hanuš Wihan, who had urged him for some time to write a concerto for his instrument, or whether it was the experience of listening to Herbert's concerto, we shall never know: the fact remains that, as a result of both or either of these Dvořák, in 1894/95, gave the world the greatest cello concerto ever written.

On 19 May 1894 Dvořák and the entire family embarked in New York, this time eastward bound, on the *S.S. Aller.* It must have been a wonderful moment for him to know that he was going back to his beloved Bohemia, for every letter which he wrote to Simrock, to his friend Göbl and others during the last period in New York speaks of his great longing for home. They

*It must be noted that, on that date, the Czech Philharmonic Orchestra first made its appearance under that name on the concert platform, but it was not until 1901 that it became an independent entity and a pure concert orchestra divorced from the opera pit.

arrived in Prague on 30 May, and there was a whole crowd of friends and officials to welcome him. Many different receptions were laid on for him, but Dvořák avoided as many as he could without offending too many susceptibilities: all he wanted was to get back to Vysoká. He arrived there on 4 June and was received by villagers and friends with a torchlight procession – a gesture which, considering his character, was probably much more to his liking than official receptions and orations. Most of this summer he spent in Vysoká, enjoying his pigeons, the Bohemian countryside, and nature in general. In late July he finished the revision of *Dimitrij*, but as far as original compositions are concerned, this period of leisure produced only two results: the eight Humoresques for Piano (op.101) and two little piano pieces. The Humoresques are a true masterpiece as a set of short piano pieces, and Simrock was glad to pay a fair-sized price for them. It is one of these vagaries of public taste that only one of them, No.7 in G flat, became what we can describe as a 'hit', and on that one alone Simrock must have made a small fortune. Everybody knows it even nowadays in all sorts of arrangements, generally transposed to G, and I would not be surprised to find a version of it for piccolo flute and double bassoon – but unfortunately it is least known in its original form for piano. The other Humoresques are just as enchanting and likeable, but somehow or other it is only No.7 which caught the public fancy.

Dvořák's happy days in Vysoká came to an end shortly after his 53rd birthday, 8 September 1894. To mark the occasion he had given the village church an organ (thirty years earlier he did not have enough money to hire himself an upright piano!) and on his birthday he played that organ himself at its consecration. Four days later he was off first to Sychrov (where presumably he visited friend Göbl) and Semily, and then on to Prague where he attended concerts of his own chamber music and conducted the Prague first performance of his Symphony in E minor on 13 October. Then, on 16 October 1894, he went to Hamburg, where he saw the son, Josef Bohuslav, of his old friend and teacher Josef Foerster, and on 18 October he embarked on his last voyage to New York. Parting must have been very difficult for him at that time. He had to leave Bohemia again to return to New York, and he knew that there were troubles and arguments ahead with Mrs. Thurber, financial and otherwise. This time, as his stay was to be a short one, he was only accompanied by his wife and his second son Otakar, so once again the family was split up.

The three of them reached New York on 26 October 1894, and the very next day Dvořák was made an Honorary Member of the Czech National Theatre Society of Brno. A few days later he was also made an Honorary Member of the Philharmonic Society of New York. Whether these honours greatly uplifted him or whether he just took them for granted, we do not know. Of course, his works continued to be played everywhere, and he himself resumed his duties as director of the National Conservatory on 1 November 1894. There is nothing to report of this third session except that he spent all his free time composing the Cello Concerto in B minor.

This Cello Concerto (op.104) is one of Dvořák's greatest and most important works and cannot be dealt with cursorily. It is the last of Dvořák's three full-length concertos (if we disregard the early attempt at a cello concerto in 1865) and, continuing the achievement of his Piano and his Violin Concerto, it pursues that line which begins with the Beethoven E flat Piano Concerto – these are no longer vehicles for a soloist's virtuosity, nor some sort of struggle between soloist and orchestra; they are all symphonically conceived with the solo instrument, despite its enormous, prominent and technically difficult part, being integrated into the musical whole – the soloist is only *primus inter pares*. Contrary to the two earlier concertos, however, where he had restricted himself to a classical orchestra, he now introduces trombones and tuba as well as a piccolo flute and a triangle. Perhaps this was prompted by the Victor Herbert Cello Concerto which he had heard in April 1894.

He began the sketch on 8 November 1894, and at first he envisaged the work in the key of D minor. The score of the whole Concerto in its first version was completed on 9 February 1895 – the 10th birthday of his son Otakar, as Dvořák himself noted on the title page. While at work the news reached him in New York that his sister-in-law Josefina was seriously ill. It would appear that his feeling for his first great love had never completely died. This accounts for the inclusion of the beginning of the first of his Four Songs (op.82), 'Leave me alone', in the second movement of the Concerto, for this song had always been a particular favourite of Josefina. Later in 1895, on 27 May and just one month after his return to Bohemia, Josefina died, and as a tribute to her he altered the Coda of the Finale, once more recalling this song.

He dedicated the work to Hanuš Wihan, but unfortunately there was considerable disagreement between Dvořák and Wihan who wanted certain passages altered and even took it upon himself to compose a cadenza for the Finale. Dvořák accepted some of Wihan's alterations in the solo part of the first movement, but for the rest he was adamant, and it is worth quoting in full what he wrote to Simrock on 3 October:

'I have had some differences of opinion with Friend Wihan over a number of places. I don't like some of the passages – and I must insist on my work being printed as I wrote it. The passages in question can be printed in two versions, an *easier* and a *more difficult* version. I shall only give you the work if you promise not to allow *anybody* to make changes – Friend Wihan not excepted – without my *knowledge* and *consent* – and also not the cadenza that Wihan has added to the last movement. There is no cadenza in the last movement either in the score or in the piano arrangement. I told Wihan straight away when he showed it to me that it was impossible to stick such a bit on. The Finale closes gradually diminuendo, like a sigh, with reminiscences of the 1st and 2nd movements – the solo dies down to *pp*, then swells

again, and the last bars are taken up by the orchestra and
the whole concludes in a stormy mood. That is my idea
and I cannot depart from it.'

Owing to circumstances – as we shall see later – it was not to
be Wihan who gave the work its first performance. But in this
connection we must mention Brahms, who had then already
written his great Double Concerto in A minor for Violin and
Cello. Donald Tovey in his *Essays in Musical Analysis,* Vol III,
tells of a meeting with the cellist Hausmann, from whom he had
the following story:

'. . . On perhaps the last occasion on which Hausmann
called upon Brahms in Vienna he found him reading a
score that had just been sent him. Brahms, before he
would talk of anything else, must first give vent to his
grumble: "Why on earth didn't I know that one could
write a violoncello concerto like this? If I had only known,
I would have written one long ago!" '

During these last six months in America in 1894/95 Dvořák
appears to have done no conducting whatsoever – apart,
presumably, from his rehearsals with the Conservatory
Orchestra. The Cello Concerto is the last composition which
he completed in New York, but while at work on it he
orchestrated five of the ten Biblical Songs as well as the Suite in
A as mentioned earlier. Being a conscientious person, he also
tried again to write an opera on *Hiawatha,* but as all librettos
submitted to him were below standard these attempts
remained abortive. During the time of his third term in office in
New York the Kneisel Quartet gave their fiftieth performance
of his 'American' Quartet in F, but what probably gave him the
greatest pleasure was when, on 16 February 1895, he was
made an Honorary Member of the *Gesellschaft der Musik-
freunde* in Vienna, a signal honour indeed! Apart from all that,
his life went on in its routine manner. He did his teaching, and
for the rest of it he started work on a String Quartet in A flat,
but only got as far as writing part of the first movement. He also

valiantly resisted all attempts by the indefatigable Mrs.
Thurber, who was trying most assiduously to entice him back
to America for a fourth session as Director of the
Conservatory.

   Together with Anna and Otakar he left America on 16 April
1895, although according to his contract Mrs. Thurber would
have been entitled to his services up to the end of the month.
However, as she was badly in arrears with the payments of his
salary he probably had few scruples in cutting short his stay.
He was never to return to America again, and by some quirk of
fate the three Dvořáks returned to Europe on the very same
ship which had first taken them across the Atlantic in 1892: the
S.S. Saale.

INTERLUDIUM IV:
FROM THE WORKSHOP

Dvořák was not the kind of man to write long effusions about his work, his purpose, or his methods *à la* Wagner, so we have hardly any first-hand information from him apart from the odd mention he makes in letters to his really close friends such as Göbl. For the rest of it we must rely on the internal evidence we possess through the medium of his sketches and his scores, as well as the invaluable reminiscences of Kovařík and several passages in the memoirs of his pupils.

The fact that Dvořák was first and foremost a melodist has been stressed often enough, and this appears to have reflected strongly on his process of composition: those sections of a work which were essentially melodically inspired were set down by him in one uninterrupted flow and came into being from the very first almost in their final form. Where he had to exert himself making sketch after sketch and ever revising, were the transitional passages, where at times he really had to work hard to make those sections which had come so natural to him coalesce into an organic entity. His pupil Josef Michl in his 'My first lesson with Dvořák' tells us that one of his fellow-pupils, on hearing some melodic fragment, exclaimed: 'That would be lovely!'. Dvořák replied rather sharply:

'Of course it would be lovely, but the thing is *to do it*. To have a lovely thought is nothing so remarkable. A thought comes of itself, and if it is fine and great it is not our merit. *But to carry out a thought well and make something great of it, that is the most difficult thing, that is in fact – ART!'*

In this context it is also worth noting what Emil Koberg, in his memoirs, quotes Dvořák as having said to him:

> 'Well, it is difficult to believe anything. They like something today and jeer at it tomorrow. I've already had a taste of that. And it's particularly hard for the Czech musician. Only now are they giving Smetana a real chance, long after his death. So not even the greatest success causes me to become conceited. I work with integrity and do best in that way. This conviction gives me the greatest satisfaction. If I have created something for posterity, then my devotion to music and work of many years will have fulfilled its most splendid purpose. However, I distrust popularity.'

He was a tireless worker, and composition for him was something compulsive, something of an obsession. From Kovařík's accounts we know that he was difficult to get on with and disgruntled whenever there was no work in progress, irritable and bad-tempered, but the moment an inspiration struck him, a new composition had taken a firm hold on his mind, then he was

> '. . . absorbed in his work, he took no heed whether the earth turned from east to west or the other way about, worked calmly and contentedly, was glad when his work went forward satisfactorily, and if, as he was in the habit of saying, "he brought something off", then he was in a particularly good mood; a truly delightful person, always smiling and joking'.

As a sidelight it is perhaps worth mentioning once more that, in a sense like Brahms, he was in the habit of writing works in the first instance for piano, for piano duet, or for a voice or solo instrument with piano accompaniment which he later orchestrated. Prime examples in point are the Slavonic Dances and the Legends, the Suite in A, the Biblical Songs, as well as a number of short pieces for violin or cello and piano. – All this may seem pretty meagre information, but that is all we have, apart from Dvořák's American sketch books, and all they seem to indicate is, again, that his first and foremost preoccupation was with *melody*.

Many great musicians, composers and performers alike, have been failures as teachers, just as many great teachers did not achieve anything remarkable as practising musicians. By all accounts Dvořák must have been an exceedingly fine teacher, but in a completely unorthodox manner, as is almost to be expected. He worked as the spirit moved him and did not care a fig if he wreaked havoc with the Conservatorium time-table, even though it drove his more bureaucratic colleagues to distraction. In the same way in which his inspiration as a composer was dictated by his affinity with his theme, his inspiration as a teacher was dictated by the personal affinity with his pupils, and in the case of teaching such an affinity is always a two-way relationship. Some pupils simply could not find any contact with him, this inexplicable spiritual inter-relation which is so absolutely essential between master and pupil, and they soon disappeared from the scene of their own volition or were discarded by Dvořák himself. But for those who were, in present-day terminology, 'on the same wavelength', he was, in the words of Oskar Nedbal, 'a comrade on the one hand, a God on the other', and they stuck to him to the death.

It must be remembered that Dvořák, in the course of his own musical training, had never received official instruction in the subjects of composition or orchestration: in both these fields he was entirely self-taught. But two things stood him in good stead. One was his very wide experience as an orchestral player. Once, when complimented on his orchestration, he said that 'any good conductor' – i.e. any musician intimately versed in orchestral procedure – could orchestrate as well as he. (A fine statement, but unfortunately not true.) The other is that, throughout his life, he always interested himself and studied the compostitions of the Great, and all his students agreed that he knew the works from Bach and Handel up to Wagner and Liszt in detail, that he could sit down at the drop of a hat and play examples from these masterworks at the piano from memory. In addition, he always kept abreast with what was going on in the world of music around him and took a lively interest in, for example, the music of Bruckner and the young Richard Strauss.

In class he must have been a very hard taskmaster who suffered no slovenliness and slipshod work. To him music was a serious matter, and he expected his students to take the same serious attitude towards it. Suk once said: 'Sometimes he drives us to the verge of tears, but we learn so much from him', and Josef Michl complains of Dvořák's volatile nature and occasional moodiness: in one lesson he might lay something down as the law and then flatly contradict himself on the following day. But this is the nature of a genius and, let us admit it, people of genius sometimes are not all that easy to get on with! Yet even when he lost his temper the storm was soon over, and with his innate kindliness he quickly regretted his outburst. His pupil Pellegrini tells a delightful story in his personal memoirs:

'. . . On one occasion he exclaimed: "You are a big ass", when handing back some work. He then noticed that the unfortunate youth, having picked up his hat and coat, was quietly leaving the classroom. Dashing after him, he brought him back with the words: "You are not a big ass". When the class was over, Dvořák went up to the student and whispered almost inaudibly: "But you are a little one".'

His teaching method was a strange mixture of adherence to classical precepts and encouragement of originality. On the one hand, if a student brought him a piece of homework, music written 'in the style of so-and-so', he would reject it out of hand,

and Michl quotes Dvořák as saying: 'Only he is a true composer who creates something truly original.' But on the other hand he was equally adamant in drumming into his pupils a sense of reverence for the great masters of the past. Apparently he was given to directing some rather enigmatic questions at his pupils, and according to Dolanský he once asked the class in general: 'What is Mozart?'. He got all sorts of answers, but none of them proved satisfactory. He raised his voice and asked the question again. Then Dvořák's temperament got the better of him, and he grabbed the pupil nearest to him by his coat sleeve, dragged him to the window and pointed heavenwards: 'Can't you see anything?' When the poor fellow kept stammering and stuttering, Dvořák bawled out: 'Well, remember: MOZART IS SUNSHINE!'.

One last point regarding Dvořák's methods as a teacher is perhaps worth mentioning. He was not one of those teachers who went through his student's composition exercises with a red pencil, but compelled them to think for themselves. He would sit down at the piano and play their exercises to them once, twice, three times over without saying a word, expecting them to hear the deficiencies themselves. The only thing he might possibly concede was to make slight alterations at subsequent play-throughs to stir their imagination. As he said himself, and quite rightly so: 'What good would it be to you if I were to write it the way it should be! It wouldn't be yours then, and every musician worth his salt would know that somebody had put it right for you. Anybody who wants to compose must get accustomed to think and work independently!'

It must be admitted, however, that in certain ways Dvořák also made use of his students. On occasion he put them to work on his own account and made them copy out his scores, the necessary orchestral parts, prepare piano reductions and vocal scores – all those chores which form part and parcel of a composer's profession. While in Prague, I was told a delightful story, but I cannot vouch for its authenticity. Apparently Josef Suk had travelled out to Vysoká to court his sweetheart Otilie. But before he could get started, Papa Dvořák dragged him into the little garden pavilion and got him to help copy out parts for some new work which was about to have its first performance. From Suk's point of view – and probably Otilie's too – a complete waste of a visit!

So here we have a thumb-nail sketch of Dvořák at work, both as composer and teacher. His methods as a teacher suited some and did not suit others, and they were unorthodox in the extreme. But the end justifies the means, and the fact remains that from Dvořák's composition class stemmed many of the great composers who distinguished themselves in Czech music at the turn of the nineteenth century, pre-eminently Josef Suk and Vítězslav Novák.

THE FINAL YEARS

Dvořák together with his wife and Otakar arrived back in Prague on 27 April 1895. This time his return was without any 'pomp and circumstance', for he had been careful to avoid spreading the news of his home-coming. Only a few friends knew about it, and after attending a performance of *Dimitrij* on 19 May at the National Theatre he hastily retreated to Vysoká. There, unhappily, a great sorrow awaited him: his first love Josefina Čermáková-Kaunicová died on 27 May 1895, and two days later he attended her funeral. (Her husband, Count Kaunic, incidentally, survived her by more than eighteen years.) During the last years remaining to him Dvořák travelled abroad very little: he went to Vienna on several occasions, paid a single visit to Berlin and Budapest, and the longest journey he undertook was his ninth and last trip to London in 1896; apart from that he hardly left the boundaries of his native land.

After returning to Bohemia he felt that he had to re-integrate himself into the musical and artistic life of his country, having been absent for so long. That he immediately resumed contact again with his friends and fellow-musicians goes without saying, but he also joined a regular Friday evening circle at the Hlávkas, where men of intellect, culture and science met regularly. But basically he spent the summer of 1895 in

Vysoká and, by Dvořák's standards, it was a lazy one. He embarked on no new compositions, although he revised the Coda of the Finale of his Cello Concerto and adapted his Oratorio 'St. Ludmila' for stage performance – but such revisions did not count as 'work' in Dvořák's eyes, and he was quite justified in writing to Hanuš Wihan in July 1895:

> '. . . Since I have come back from America I have not put pen to paper, and so the new Quartet begun in New York is still not finished.
>
> The first movement unfinished and of the others not even the beginnings! Here at Vysoká I grudge the time and prefer to enjoy the beauties of the countryside.'

Within Bohemia he moved about a good deal, visiting old friends such as Rus, Hlávka, Kaán and others, probably Göbl as well, and on two occasions (in May and in October) he went to Carlsbad to meet Simrock and Hanslick. Apart from all that, we can assume with certainty that he also renewed his contacts with the railway officials and engine drivers at the Prague Station and checked up on the numbers of the locomotives going in and out.

On 1 November Dvořák resumed his duties as Professor at the Prague Conservatorium, and with the resumption of those duties his creative urge seems also to have returned. He first composed what is generally considered his last string quartet (but is not), the one in G (op.106) which he wrote between 11 November and 9 December 1895. It is, to my mind, undoubtedly the greatest of all his string quartets, but it has never attained the popularity which its quality deserves, and certain other chamber works of his, though much inferior, have caught the audiences' favour to a far greater extent. In passing it is also amusing that, had he written the G major Quartet No. 13 in America, everybody would pounce on its pentatonic tendencies and attribute its melodies to Negro or Red Indian folk-music, whereas in actual fact it is the most fervent Bohemian thanksgiving at being back in his homeland. Immediately afterwards, on 12 December 1895, he went back

to the String Quartet No. 14 in A flat (op.105) of which he had
written the beginning of the first movement – a matter of 100
bars or so – in America and completed it by the end of 1895 –
on 30 December, to be exact.

Little more can be said about that year 1895. In December
(sometime between the 12th and the 18th) he took a short trip
to Vienna to see Brahms and Richter, and Christmas he spent
at home. The following excerpt from a letter to Göbl, dated 23
December 1895, sums it all up:

'. . . We are all, thanks be to God, well and rejoice to be
able, after three years, to spend a happy and joyous
Christmas in Bohemia! How different it was for us last
year in America, when we were far away in foreign parts
and separated from all our children and friends! But God
has been pleased to grant us this happy moment and so
we all feel inexpressibly glad!

I am now working very hard. I work so easily and
everything goes ahead so well that I could not wish it
better. I have just finished a new G major Quartet and
now again am finishing a second in A flat major. Two
movements are quite complete and I am just writing the
Andante, and expect to be finished with it after the
holidays. . . .'

1896 then started with that concert in Prague on 4 January in
which he conducted a programme of his own works, including
the first performance of the first five Biblical Songs in their
orchestral garb.

When, two days before the end of the year 1895, Dvořák
finished the composition of his last string quartet, he
inexplicably entered into a new phase as a composer, a phase
which was to last to the end of his days. Not only was this
String Quartet in A flat his very last chamber work, but it was
also the last piece of *absolute* music he ever composed. It is
true that his great dream had always been to write a truly

successful opera, but up to now his reputation really rested on his accomplishments as a composer of symphonies, concertos, and chamber works. It is also true that in the days of his youth, when he worked as a viola player in the orchestra, he fell under the influence of Liszt and Wagner, and those composers put a strong and undeniable stamp on his early compositions. As time went on , he came more and more under the spell of the classics, particularly Beethoven and Schubert, and when Brahms entered his life this trend became even more pronounced. Even though at times – particular instances being the *Dumky* Trio and the G major Symphony – he went his own 'Bohemian' ways and strayed from the strict classical form, there is no denying that he followed the rules and precepts of classical composition. Then, at the beginning of 1896, there is a complete *volte face*: he turned away from the absolute music which he had written in the past and suddenly followed the dictates of the Neo-German school. In those last eight and a half years of his life there were no further chamber works, no more symphonies – he gave the world only symphonic poems and operas apart from one or two minor, occasional compositions.

Before we plunge into this period, we must look at some more biographical facts. In February 1896 he went to Vienna to be present at the Viennese première, conducted by Hans Richter, of his 'New World' Symphony. Again the success was tremendous, and he could proudly write to Simrock on 19 February:

'. . . I was in Vienna on the 16th February 1896. Richter sent me a telegram. It was a great success and the audience gave me a grand reception. I sat with Brahms in the Director's box. – The applause was so great that I had to bow from the box three times after the *Largo* and again three times after the *Scherzo*, and after the Finale I had to go down to the hall, and show myself to the appreciative audience from the platform. I have never known such a success in Vienna. I thank God for it!'

There is also the likelihood that in February 1896, after his return from Vienna, Bronislav Hubermann – a pupil of Joachim – may have visited Dvořák in Prague.

Let us now go back to the Cello Concerto. Details of its composition have already been given; we know that he dedicated it to Wihan, and also that there had been some differences of opinion between composer and dedicatee. It has often been assumed that these minor divergencies of opinion prevented Wihan from being the soloist in the concerto at the first performance in London. As a result of more recent findings it is now clear that the real reason was much more prosaic: a clash or overlapping of dates. The Philharmonic Society of London, in order to make the first performance possible under Dvořák's direction, suggested the cellist Leo Stern as soloist, and after a certain amount of correspondence to and fro Dvořák, with Wihan's consent, agreed. As a result Stern came to Prague in late January 1896 to study the concerto with Dvořák in person, and so Dvořák went to London with Otilie to conduct the first performance of the Cello Concerto with Stern as soloist. At this concert at the Queen's Hall on 19th March Dvořák also directed a performance of his Symphony No.8 as well as the Five Biblical Songs. Mackenzie took the baton for the remainder of the programme which included Beethoven's Piano Concerto in E flat with Emil Sauer as soloist and some further items. With my built-in conductor's mentality I cannot help adding up durations: in that programme the music alone totals about 135 minutes, not counting the 'further items'. The piano also had to be shifted, there were applause and acknowledgements, plus at least one interval. One has to admire the stamina of the audiences in those days!

He duly received the ovations to which he was accustomed in England, but he was not happy; the weather was London's worst, he complained about the English food and so, apart from his success as a musician, he was as disillusioned with London as he had been in 1894 on his return to New York. This is probably neither the fault of London nor of New York, but simply has its roots in the fact that he had fallen back into his familiar routine in Prague and his Vysoká and just did not like travelling abroad any more. I am sure that this also was the underlying reason why, when he went to Vienna for a week at the end of March in 1896, he turned down Brahms' offer of a Professorship at the Vienna Conservatorium.

Let us now consider those symphonic poems which Dvořák composed in 1896/97 within the space of about 22 months. It is symptomatic that, from the time he finished his last two string quartets to his dying day, he never touched a subject which was not related to Bohemian legend and history, with the exception of his very last work – the opera *Armida*. It is almost as though he intended to complete his life's work as a Czech musician.

For the first four of these tone poems he drew on ballads by the poet Karel Jaromír Erben, a fervent nationalist like Dvořák who had already provided the text for the Oratorio 'The Spectre's Bride'. Dvořák selected four of these ballads which are all firmly anchored in Bohemian mythology and, consequently (as is the habit of almost all myths and legends) are macabre in subject and mood: they all deal with such emanations as goblins and witches, and usually end in death and bloodshed for the human beings who get themselves involved with the supernatural. The first three of these ballads Dvořák set to music between 6 January and 25 April 1896, and he followed a rather uncharacteristic course by first sketching *Vodník* ('The Water Goblin'), *Polednice* ('The Noon Witch') and *Zlatý kolovrat* ('The Golden Spinning Wheel') within 16 days and then returning to the beginning, orchestrating each in turn. This is strange, because as a rule he devoted himself to one major work at a time, and even in the case of those three Overtures which form a cycle he sketched and orchestrated each on its own – and there is nothing cyclic about these tone poems except that they are all related to the legends of his native land. The other striking thing is that he went to great lengths in his letters to give what one might call a 'blow-by-blow account' of the course of the action clearly based on Erben's poems. He even went so far as to cite precise bar numbers, tonalities, and instruments. He had never before followed so faithfully the favourite methods of the Neo-Germans – the nearest he had ever come to it was in his Overture *Othello*. The last ot the four Symphonic Poems based on the poems of Erben was *Holoubek* ('The Wild Dove') which he wrote in October /November 1896, and everything which has been said about the earlier three also applies to this one. Lastly came a fifth, *Písen Bohatýrská* ('Hero's Song') which he composed between 4 August and 25 October 1897 and which is not based on any specific programme, but is quite clearly intended as a piece of musical autobiography in the same way as Richard Strauss' *Ein Heldenleben,* completed roughly a year later.

These five works which, incidentally, are the last works for orchestra – or, indeed, for any purely instrumental combination – which Dvořák ever put down on paper must have meant a great deal to him, for he did not allow work on these tone poems to be interrupted by any other composition except for the final revision (during most of 1897) of his opera *Jacobín*. From then onward followed only a flow of operas. Dvořák must have been absolutely convinced that he was right to change his course so drastically, but it also had side effects. He had always been considered a follower of the classical tradition, a fact which had become more and more firmly established through his friendship with Brahms. It is not surprising therefore that it shocked Hanslick to the very core to find that this protégé of his should suddenly veer in the direction of Liszt and Wagner – a musical world which was anathema to him. Consequently, after the 'New World' Symphony had had its first performance in Vienna, and when it was already known that Dvořák was at work on his *Vodník*, he did write very favourably about the Symphony, but added:

'. . . I cannot quite comprehend how one could choose such a ghastly theme, which is revolting to every artistically sensitive person, as the topic for a musical representation. . . .

I am afraid that with this detailed programmatic music Dvořák has stepped onto a slippery slope which, in the end, leads directly to – Richard Strauss. . . .

I just cannot accept that I must now put Dvořák . . . on one level with Richard Strauss; he is a true musician who has proved a hundred times that he needs no programme and no description to enchant us through the medium of pure, absolute music. . . . But after "The Water Goblin" a little friendly warning perhaps does not come amiss.'*

These tone poems, written one after another, stand out as a unique feature in Dvořák's entire output. What is one to say about them? That Dvořák was a masterly craftsman, composer and orchestrator goes without saying. That he had a fund of melodic invention has been stressed often enough – far too often, in fact. These five works – or at least the first four of them – are a real delight, with the enchanted and enchanting atmosphere they conjure up. But are they truly great? At the risk of offending some I venture to say 'no': the true greatness of Dvořák's orchestral and instrumental compositions really lies in his symphonies and his chamber music. Dvořák was a 'romantic classic' or a 'classical romantic', as you please. But he was no extrovert, the Neo-German precepts were somehow alien to him and, with all due respect, he did not manage to scale those heights which Smetana reached in his *Má Vlast*. Nevertheless, and despite what has just been said, conductors of the time took to these tone poems and championed them. If we discount a private performance of them in Prague, 'The Golden Spinning Wheel', 'The Water Goblin', and 'The Noon Witch' all had their first performances in London, 'The Golden Spinning Wheel' under Hans Richter and the other two under Sir Henry Wood. Richter also

*Karin Stöckl/Klaus Döge: from the introduction to the score of Dvořák Symphony No.9 (Goldmann/Schott, Mainz 1982).

presented two of them in Vienna, and Janáček gave the first perfomance of 'The Wild Dove' in March 1898 in Brno. But perhaps the greatest triumph for Dvořák – as far as these tone poems are concerned – was that Mahler gave the première of the 'Hero's Song' in Vienna on 4 December 1898 and that Nikisch played the work twice in Berlin and then in the Leipzig *Gewandhaus* in November 1899. It should also be noted that these tone poems found equal favour with Dvořák's publisher in Berlin: whereas Simrock had palmed him off with a measly 300 Marks for the first set of Slavonic Dances in the earlier years, he now cheerfully paid out 12,000 Marks for the first three of those tone poems.

We seem to be switching to and fro between Dvořák's artistic endeavours and the unremarkable happenings which made up his daily life. But this oscillation, confusing though it may be, is essential if we want to understand a person who was a genius on the one hand and a simple, kindly family man and nature lover on the other. Such a personality cannot be dissected with a surgeon's scalpel into its various parts such as 'the man' and 'the music'.

We last saw Dvořák on his brief visit to England on the occasion when, in March 1896, he conducted the first performance of his Cello Concerto. On his return he only spent a single day in Prague, and on March 22 he went to Vienna together with the Czech Quartet. It is the visit which has been mentioned earlier, when he was accompanied by his wife and future son-in-law Josef Suk. He visited Brahms, and it was on this occasion that Brahms offered him the Professorship at the Vienna Conservatorium. The main reason for his stay – which lasted until March 28 – was to conduct a performance of 'The Spectre's Bride' with the Llubljana Choral Society and to attend a chamber music concert on 27 March at which the Czech Quartet performed Brahms' String Sextet in B flat, Dvořák's Sextet in A and the Bruckner String Quintet. Apart from these concerts it was definitely the renewed contact with

Brahms that meant most to Dvořák, but for us nowadays it is
equally important that during those days in Vienna he also
visited Bruckner. It is the only time the two men ever met, and
from Suk's *Aus meiner Jugend* we glean the following details:

> '. . . On the evening on which the Bruckner Quintet was
> to be performed, we went before the concert to visit
> Bruckner and to invite him to the performance of his
> work. At that time Bruckner occupied the well-known
> vaulted room in the Belvedere. We found him with his
> coat off at his writing desk and we had the impression that
> this was the home of a man who lives altogether in the
> world of the spirit and for his work. He looked at us
> without a sign of recognition, with a far-away look in his
> eyes and did not at once grasp what we were wanting.
> Only after a while did he comprehend: "You want me to
> come to the concert. I can't do that. I am so often ailing
> and I have too much work. You see I am busy working at
> the *Adagio**** of the 9th and so I must stay at home today."
> When we took leave of him he was suddenly very
> touched. Tears stood in those remarkable eyes of his. He
> saw us out in his quilted vest and blew us kisses as long as
> our carriage was in sight.'

The mention of this meeting with Bruckner prompts yet
another line of thought: how are we to assess Dvořák in
relationship to Wagner and Bruckner? Everything has already
been said about the great influence which Wagner had exerted
on Dvořák in his youthful compositions, and it is also true that
in the operas of his late years he again reverted to certain
Wagnerian principles. But this raises the question: was
Dvořák ever a 'Wagnerian'? Or, for that matter, what is a
'Wagnerian'? It is true that Dvořák employed the ideas of

---

*There must be some slight error here. Bruckner completed the *Adagio* and
with it the first three complete movements of his Symphony No.9 on 30
November 1894. By the time Dvořák visited him he was already engaged on
the Finale which remained incomplete at his death on 11 October 1896.

Leitmotiv in Wagner's sense, it is true that his operas for the most part are *durchkomponiert,* 'through-composed', and it is also true that, according to Michl, he once remarked:

'. . . What Wagner did nobody did before him and nobody can take it from him. Music will go its way, will pass Wagner by, but Wagner will remain, just like the statue of that poet of whom they still learn at school today: *Homer.* And such a Homer is Wagner!' . . .

But on the other hand we must also consider the fact that Seidl, in New York, once invited him to the 'Met' for a performance of *Siegfried,* and Dvořák left the Opera House after the first act because 'he could not stand this eternal *Nibelung* rhythm any longer'. This is almost as 'un-Wagnerian' as Bruckner's remark after a performance of *Walküre*: 'Tell me, why did they burn that woman in the end?' Both Dvořák and Bruckner admired the composer and musician Wagner, each in a different way, to the point of adulation, but in the last resort they *did* not and *would* not follow his philosophical dictates.

With Bruckner we enter a different realm. Dvořák, as has been said, only met him once, and that at a time when Bruckner had but a few months more to live and was already far removed from the realities of this world: he was then only living for his last artistic effort – the Finale of the Symphony No.9. Dvořák studied Bruckner quite seriously, as we know from the article by Jiři Vysloužil (*Bruckner Jahrbuch* 1981, Linz) and he knew at least some of the symphonies from having heard them at concerts. Basically he appears to have liked Bruckner's music, though he found him (particularly in the Finale of Symphony No.8) too long-winded. These two men had so much in common: they were both products of the Austro-Hungarian Empire of the days of the 1848 revolution, they were both staunch Roman Catholics, they both came from humble ancestry, and they were both rooted in the country-side and folk-music of their native land. In addition they shared a deep love of nature. But despite all these similarities two factors put them miles apart. One of these was a musico-political factor which did not really concern them and which later times have proved to be completely irrelevant: Bruckner was stamped by Hanslick and his clique as the 'Wagnerian Symphonist', Dvořák was the Brahms protégé – and this alone in the musical world of that time made them appear irreconcilable opposites. But much more important is the fact that Bruckner lived in a spiritual world with his feet barely touching the ground, whereas Dvořák always had both feet firmly on the ground and looked up to the spiritual spheres above.

But we have digressed. After his return from Vienna Dvořák conducted the Czech Philharmonic Orchestra in the Prague première of his Cello Concerto, again with Leo Stern as soloist, then the String Quartet in A flat had its first performance at a private concert, and on the next day he travelled to Olomouc to conduct two performances of 'St.Ludmila' on 18 and 19 April 1896. Obviously he had to carry on with his teaching activities, but then came the summer recess which again he spent in Vysoká with the occasional trip up to Prague. The first of these visits was to attend the private performance, on 3 June, of the first three of the Symphonic Poems conducted by Antonín Bennewitz, which resulted in his revising the works in Vysoká, and in July he had to make the journey again to attend the graduation concert of pupils from his own as well as Karel Bendl's composition classes. About a month later he was back in Prague to visit Bendl who was then already a very sick man. Apart from that Dvořák only visited a few friends in Bohemia, among them Göbl in Sychrov. He did not start composing again until 22 October 1896, shortly after the Czech Quartet had given the first performance of the G major String Quartet in Prague and by then, of course, he was back in harness at the Conservatorium. What remained of that year was devoted to 'The Wild Dove'.

The rest of Dvořák's life continued in the way which he had chosen for himself and which he enjoyed. In March 1897 he went to Vienna briefly to see Brahms, who was then already mortally ill, for the last time. A matter of three weeks later, on 3 April, his great friend Brahms died and Dvořák returned to attend the funeral. Musically 1897 was relatively uneventful, if we ignore the fact that performances of Dvořák's works at home and abroad were becoming increasingly frequent – so much so that it now becomes superfluous to refer to them unless there is some specific reason. This spate of performances also meant that Dvořák could gradually retire from the rostrum as a conductor of his own works. As far as compositions are concerned, he spent a lot of that year on a final and thorough revision of *Jacobín*, particularly the third act, and it was in the midst of that work that he also wrote his 'Hero's Song'.

In his private life sorrow and happiness were intermingled. It is unavoidable that, when a person reaches a certain age, the days are usually past for attending weddings and christenings – sadly it is funerals which become the order of the day. In September 1897, only a few months after Brahms' death, he had to say farewell to that faithful companion of his youth, Karel Bendl, and in the years to follow he also lost his friends Zdeněk Fibich, Julius Zeyer, Fritz Simrock as well as the wife of Josef Hlávka. Somewhat later, on 14 December 1903, his mother-in-law Klotilda Čermáková died at the age of eighty, and about a fortnight after that Dvořák attended the funeral of the conductor Adolf Čech who had done so much to further his music. So, sadly, the circle of those close to Dvořák's heart dwindled. But there were joyful occasions too, and there is one which must have been a highlight. It may be recalled that Antonín and Anna were married on 17 November 1873, 33 years to the day after the wedding of Dvořák's parents. Now, on 17 November 1898, their Silver Wedding anniversary was coming up, and matters were arranged in such a way that their eldest daughter Otilie was to marry Josef Suk on the same day, making it a double event. Suk had been Dvořák's pupil, had become his friend, and was beginning to establish a reputation for himself as a composer. The two young people had been in love with each other for over three years, so that day must have been a great family occasion for all of them. Unfortunately we have no direct information as to the shape which these festivities took, nor as to the precise amount of Pilsen beer which was consumed! Just to complete the 'family news', Dvořák must also have been very happy when his second daughter Anna was married in October 1903, but the proudest moment was no doubt when Otilie gave birth to his first grandchild on 19 December 1901, just a few months after Dvořák's own 60th birthday, and this grandson was christened Josef after his father. He in turn became the father of that third Josef Suk, born in 1929, who is one of the great Czech violinists of our time.

In the professional sphere Dvořák was in great demand. As early as 1896 Mrs. Thurber had stretched out feelers to see whether she could inveigle him back to the United States, but Dvořák seems to have hedged and avoided the issue. She then tried to get him to come to New York in Spring 1898 to supervise the end-of-year examinations and to act as judge for the prize compositions. Mrs. Thurber even deputized a friend of hers, a Miss Margulies who was spending a holiday in Austria, to see Dvořák and act as a sort of envoy to persuade him to return to New York for a short spell at least. But after much discussion Dvořák would only agree to allow Mrs. Thurber the use of his name as 'Director of the National Conservatory' – in other words: just a prestige name on the headed note paper, without any other strings attached. In 1898 Dvořák also received offers from England on the part of the Philharmonic Society and the Sheffield Music Festival to return as a guest conductor but, although there was a certain amount of correspondence, nothing came of either invitation. Dvořák was too happy at home and could not be bothered to rush around in the way that is the custom of musicians nowadays.

But it was not just a question of invitations from great and famous institutions: honours were also being showered on Dvořák during those closing years, among them the greatest honours which the Austro-Hungarian Empire had in its power to bestow. In November 1897 he was appointed to succeed Brahms as a member of the Jury for awarding State Scholarships, and considering how much he himself had benefitted from this institution it must have been a cause for rejoicing for him to be able to follow in Brahms' footsteps. Also in November 1898 the Emperor of Austria awarded him the Order *Litteris et Artibus* – an award which hitherto had only been granted to one composer, Johannes Brahms himself. Then, in April 1901, he was appointed a member of the *Herrenhaus* (Senate) of the Austrian Parliament (in present-day English terms the equivalent of a Life Peer) together with the leading Czech poet Emil Frída, better known as Jaroslav Vrchlický, who had provided the libretto for 'St. Ludmila'. They duly attended the Senate in Vienna on 14 May 1901 and took the oath (in Czech) with Dvořák wearing his Order *Litteris et Artibus* – which he always described as 'my big gold platter'. It was the first and last time that Dvořák attended the House in his official capacity, and perhaps his career as a politician is best described by Josef Penížek, who reports:

'. . . Each member of the Austrian Senate had in front of him an inkpot, a sandsprinkler, blotting-paper, several pens, and several pencils, Hardmut no. 2, soft and yet not brittle, the best product of its kind. Dvořák was greatly delighted with these pencils. He took them all and put them in his pocket. Having left the Senate House, he showed his booty to his wife who was waiting for him and said: 'Look, they will be marvellous for composing!'

But he was not honoured in Vienna alone, but also in Prague. In the summer of 1901 Bennewitz, the Director of the Prague Conservatorium, went into retirement, and Dvořák was elected as his successor, an appointment which he took up on 6 July 1901, although everyone knew perfectly well that he was no administrator, and he seems to have taken his duties as Director as seriously as he took his political duties as a member of the Senate in Vienna. Fortunately for him – and for the Prague Conservatorium – he had an excellent Number

Two, Karel Knittl, who saw to all the adminstrative duties so that Dvořák was unencumbered and could concentrate on his composition class. But it should perhaps be mentioned, for this is so typical of Dvořák's innate modesty, that he never absented himself to spend a few days in Vysoká without asking Knittl's permission first – even though he, Dvořák, was the principal!

These were the outstanding events in the last years of Dvořák's life, and we must now back-track to 1897 for the minor ones and also for the last phase of his activities as a composer. In May of that year he conducted a concert of his own works with the Czech Philharmonic Orchestra in Brno, and shortly afterwards he went to Carlsbad for a meeting with Simrock. Unless the two men met once more when he went to Berlin in November 1899 – and there is no evidence of this whatsoever – this meeting in Carlsbad must have been their last. There is nothing else to report for the rest of that year which has not been told before or, indeed, until we come to 5 May 1898 when he began making the first sketches for 'The Devil and Kate'. With this begins his last and purely operatic phase. There has been much conjecture about the reasons why he turned so exclusively to opera during his last years, but for once – and this is rare – we have Dvořák's own account in the form of an interview which he gave to the Vienna daily paper *Die Reichswehr*, published on 1 March 1904, precisely two months before his death:

'. . . In the last five years I have written nothing but operas. I wanted to devote all my powers, for as long as the dear Lord gives me health, to the creation of opera. This is not, however, because of a yearning for glory as far as the stage is concerned, but simply for the reason that I consider opera to be the most suitable form for the people. The broad masses listen to this music, and very frequently, but if I compose a symphony it could take years before it would be performed here. Simrock has asked me more than once to write chamber music, but I have always refused. By now my publishers know that I will not write anything more just to please them. They bombard me with questions why I do not compose this, that, or the other; but this particular type of music does not attract me any longer. They look upon me as a Symphonist, yet I have proved many years ago that my overwhelming urge lies in the direction of dramatic creation.'

The composition of 'The Devil and Kate' occupied Dvořák with hardly any interruption until 27 February 1899. The summer of 1898 he spent mainly in Vysoká, but he also, as usual, visited some of his friends such as Dr. Kozánek in Kroměříž and Hlávka in Lužany, and in November, of course, occurred the great double event of Otilie's marriage to Suk and his own Silver Wedding. Shortly afterwards he went to Vienna to hear Gustav Mahler rehearse and give the first performance of his 'Hero's Song' on 4 December.

Once the score of 'The Devil and Kate' was finished, he still spent some five or six weeks on preparing a piano reduction, but after 12 April 1899 he did not write anything else until the beginning of the year 1900. 'The Devil and Kate' had its first performance in Prague on 23 November 1899 under the baton of Adolf Čech, but before that Dvořák paid a short visit to Berlin to hear Nikisch conduct the Berlin Philharmonic in his 'Hero's Song' and to renew the friendship with that great conductor which he had formed in Boston seven years earlier. Also, in December 1899, he went to Budapest for the second and last time in his life to take part as pianist in a concert of chamber music of his own. On the following day, 20 December, he conducted an orchestral concert which included the 'Hero's Song' and the Cello Concerto, and this time it was Hanuš Wihan who was the soloist. He was back in Prague in time to celebrate Christmas with the family.

One gets the feeling that somehow or other he was irked by this long period of inactivity, for all he was really waiting for after the enormous success of 'The Devil and Kate' was a new libretto. In the early months he busied himself with preparing a piano reduction of the second version of 'King and Charcoal Burner', and he made some odd sketches which never came to anything. The only work he composed was a 'Festive Ode' in honour of the 70th birthday of Dr. Tragy, the former Director and now Vice President of the Prague Conservatorium, in April 1900. On 4 April he appeared on the rostrum as a conductor for the last time in a public concert with the Czech Philharmonic, and the programme – presumably of his own choosing – consisted of works by Brahms, Schubert and Beethoven, 'The Wild Dove' being the only composition of his own. This was an entirely new thing for Dvořák, for up to then he had conducted only his own works.*

Dvořák was overjoyed when he got hold of Kvapil's libretto for *Rusalka*. He took to it immediately, for this sort of fairy tale subject was exactly what enchanted him at this period, and from 21 April until 27 November 1900 nothing else could occupy his mind for long. Even a concert under Hans Richter by the Berlin Philharmonic Orchestra in Prague did not greatly interrupt him, though Richter visited Dvořák on that occasion, and with the exception of a visit in June to his daughter Otilie and Josef Suk he just moved backwards and forwards between Prague and Vysoká. The opera was immediately accepted by the National Theatre; Dvořák attended many of the rehearsals, and the first night (conducted by Karel Kovařovic on 31 March 1901) was a triumph such as Dvořák had never witnessed in the opera house, not even with 'The Devil and Kate' – and rightly so, for *Rusalka* must be acknowledged to be Dvořák's masterpiece, the greatest opera to emerge from the pen of a Bohemian composer since Smetana and unmatched by any other composer from the Czech Lands until it came to the turn of Janáček.

It was shortly after this première that Dvořák was appointed

*Although these statements are basically correct, it must be admitted that we do not know what works he played through with the Orchestra of the National Conservatory in New York; and also it is true that, on 29 May 1900, he himself conducted the 'Festive Ode' for Dr. Tragy, but this was only before an invited audience.

a Member of the Senate, and Nikisch with the Berlin Philharmonic visited Prague. At their concert at the Rudolfinum on 15 April 1901 Dvořák's 'The Wild Dove' formed part of the programme, and then Dvořák went to Vienna for that famous session in the Senate when he pinched the pencils. Only a week later, on about 22 May 1901, he was back in Vienna to discuss the possibility of a performance of *Rusalka* with Gustav Mahler. Despite talks and much correspondence between the two men, the sad fact remains that Vienna did not hear *Rusalka* until the autumn of 1910, when the Brno Opera Company performed it there.

On 8 September 1901 Dvořák turned 60. He was by now the 'Grand Old Man' of Czech music, and the whole of Prague and Bohemia made preparations to celebrate the event on a lavish scale – just the sort of thing he loathed. The actual birthday he dodged quite simply by going to Vienna so as to deliver the score of *Rusalka* to Mahler in person. However annoyed he may have been about all the fuss it must still have given him a warm glow of satisfaction that the National Theatre, in his honour, staged no less than six of his operas* and finally followed this up with the first stage performance of 'St. Ludmila'. Nor can it have left him unmoved when, though several weeks after his actual birthday, he was given a torchlight procession and had a serenade played in the street below his flat with vociferous shouts of 'Long Live Dvořák!' There were various other receptions and banquets in his honour which he could not avoid, but he is reported to have said something to the effect that he had survived much in his life and would probably survive this as well, and on more than one occasion he was heard to say: 'Is all this really necessary?'

What concerned him much more was the fact that he could not find a suitable libretto for his next opera. True, he seriously considered a subject by Svatopluk Čech, entitled 'The Smith of Lešetín' (*Zpěv z Lešetínského Kováře*) but got no further than composing a single song from this text in August 1901.

*'The Stubborn Lovers', 'The Cunning Peasant', *Dimitrij*, *Jacobín*, 'The Devil and Kate' and *Rusalka*.

Finally, in March 1902, he settled on a text by Jaroslav Vrchlický, *Armida*, which was a really unfortunate choice. The fact remains that he was extremely depressed by the lack of inspiration and his resulting inactivity, which can be clearly seen from a letter which he wrote to Kozánek on 11 February 1902:

> 'For more than fourteen months I have done *no work* and been unable *to make up my mind*, and I don't know how long this state of affairs will continue.'

He worked on *Armida* incessantly from March 1902 until 23 August 1903. When it came to the première on 25 March 1904, Dvořák attended, but because he was already seriously ill he was compelled to leave the performance before the end. Perhaps this was just as well, for it spared him the embarrassing experience of a less than wholehearted reception. There was that polite applause which we know so well as a token of respect for an honoured Master, but which basically signals a complete and utter flop.

All that remains is to relate a few personal details of events which took place at the end of Dvořák's life. He continued to spend his day, as far as his health would permit, in the way to which he was accustomed. In March 1903 Grieg came to visit him in those same rooms in the Žitná which had already provided a welcome for Brahms, Tchaikovsky and many others, and in October 1903 his second daughter, Anna, got married. His health had always been fairly robust, but it started to fail during the winter of 1903/04. This has been ascribed to various causes, ranging from the vascular and sclerotic to kidney trouble and uraemia. Whatever the causes may have been, he was a sick man, and the doctors tried their best to keep him to his room and force him to rest. However, on 30 March 1904 he felt an overwhelming urge to take a walk to the Prague railway station to look at some locomotives. As a result he caught a chill which confined him to his bed, and so he was unable on 3 April to attend a Music Festival which was devoted entirely to his own works. By 18 April his condition had deteriorated, but on 1 May he felt well enough to get up for the midday meal and preside again at the head of the family table. From what we know he ate his soup with relish, but then he collapsed and was taken to his room. By the time the doctor arrived, Antonín Dvořák was dead.

CODA

DVOŘÁK IS DEAD – this news travelled like wildfire through the entire musical world, both at home and abroad. The people of Prague only realized what had happened in the evening of that May Day 1904, when they found the auditorium of the National Theatre draped in black. Expressions of sympathy and condolences poured in from all over the world, and the customary ceremonial of obsequies was set in motion. On the following day, 2 May, the Czech Academy held a commemorative session, and three days later thousands lined the route of the funeral procession. As it passed the National Theatre, the *Introit* of the Dvořák *Requiem* was played from the colonnade at the top of the steps; then the sombre cortège wended its way up the hill to the cemetery of Vyšehrad, that cemetery which Czechoslovakia reserves for the Greatest of its Great. There, on 5 May, Antonín Dvořák was laid to rest. A memorial service was held two days later in the Týn Church to the strains of Mozart's *Requiem* – Mozart, who for Dvořák was pure sunshine.

With Dvořák's death the world in general and his relatives and friends in particular lost a kindly, friendly, easy-going, and simple man. However, the word 'simple' is not to be misconstrued as a

synonym for 'uneducated': at Česká Kamenice he had
obtained his *Abitur* (the School Leaving Certificate) and
learned about Homer and the classics, even though he did not
study Latin; he was well versed in Shakespeare, and in later life
he was closely associated with academics – lawyers and
doctors – and it is a well-known fact that the members of such
professions do not suffer fools gladly. If any proof be needed of
Dvořák's ability to express himself by means of the written
word, the reader's attention is drawn to the articles which he
wrote for the New York press on a variety of musical topics,
particularly his article on Franz Schubert which was published
in *The Century Illustrated Monthly Magazine*, New York,
1894.

He was a man of the people and liked his fellow human
beings. We have heard a great deal about his many friends in
various walks of life, and someone might be tempted to ask:
'And who were his enemies?' The answer is simple: Dvořák
may have had differences with Simrock and Mrs. Thurber, and
he may at times have been short-tempered with his pupils and
others, but the fact remains that in all the documentary
evidence I can find no proof of Dvořák ever having had a real
enemy. When he flew into a temper or had a quarrel these
outbursts were more a matter of impatience than of genuine
rage, and he was always quick to apologize and restore peace.
All this is the more amazing as envy is the order of the day
among musicians. No doubt some composers may have
envied Dvořák his success and some critics may at times have
been less than complimentary but, reading through the
information we possess, I can find no trace of any actual
hostility.

In order to put a musician, especially a composer, in his
proper perspective it is necessary to consider him in
relationship to his contemporaries. The two 'Neo-Germans'
who influenced him so greatly – Liszt and Wagner – were
roughly a generation older than himself, if we take three
decades as being a generation gap. Smetana and Bruckner
were seventeen years, Brahms eight years his seniors,

Tchaikovsky was born one year before him, and Dvořák was already nineteen years old when Gustav Mahler was born. At one time there was a great deal of argument as to who was the greater: Smetana or Dvořák. Such arguments are as futile and nonsensical as a long discussion about the relative 'greatness' of, say, Bach and Handel, or Haydn and Mozart. There is an apocryphal story that someone asked Goethe whether he considered himself or Schiller, who was his friend, to be the greater. Goethe reputedly answered: 'Now don't you worry about that. Just be happy that you've got two such fine chaps as us!' In the same way Smetana and Dvořák are the two overtowering bastions of Czech music of the 19th century, and that really sums it up.

Of course Smetana and Dvořák *were* different, for Dvořák always had the classical concept in his mind from the very outset up to the time that he embarked on his tone poems. Nevertheless he was always a full-blooded romantic and, like Bruckner, Brahms and Tchaikovsky, he tried to re-discipline the diffuseness into which the Neo-Germans had drifted into classical form without sacrificing that personal element of utterance which characterizes the romantics. It must be admitted that Dvořák's music has the true warmth and pulsating heart of the 'simple Bohemian musician' – in this particular sense he is probably the greatest Bohemian composer up to the present day. For all that, while being perfectly well aware of his worth, he never allowed his self-esteem to go to his head or make him arrogant.

In his music he combined inspiration and craftsmanship to a masterly degree, but the greatest feature is his melodic inventiveness, a source which never seemed to dry up. Composers of a later day, especially composers of light music, have turned to Dvořák as to a veritable 'reference library', but this is a fate shared by many others. The story goes that Chopin once referred to such plagiarism and said that if anyone should ever steal one of his tunes he would turn in his grave – he is now jocularly known as the 'rotating Chopin'. I think that Dvořák would just smile in his grave and regard it as a compliment!

The quantity of Dvořák's musical output, if it does not quite compare with that of Mozart or Schubert, is still impressive, and it is a matter of regret that so much of it has fallen into neglect because of the virtual disappearance of music-making in the home and because of a different concept of programme-building. For this reason there are many charming works such as the Moravian Duets, the piano pieces, and the shorter *concertante* works such as the Romance and Mazurek for Violin and Orchestra as well as the G minor Rondo and *Klid* for Cello and Orchestra which we rarely hear in public, but to a certain extent the mechanical media – radio and gramophone records – compensate for this. Granted, the 'New World' Symphony, the Slavonic Dances, the Cello Concerto are still the all-time favourites with audiences, but those who love these works should also seek out the other compositions, for they are equally enjoyable. Dvořák was a devout Christian, a Bohemian steeped in his native soil and folk-music, and one could well place the same epigraph on his entire musical output which Beethoven wrote over the score of his *Missa Solemnis:*

From the Heart – may it go to the Heart!

APPENDICES

Appendix I
The Numbering of Dvořák's Compositions

This is a two-fold problem, beset with many difficulties. First of all we must consider the numbers given to the symphonies. All nine of them are now available in the Complete Edition (CE) of Dvořák's works which is being published in Prague under the auspices of the Antonín Dvořák Society, but there is still much bewilderment in the minds of the general public caused by the old numbering to which all but the youngest music lovers have so long been accustomed. Obviously, in the CE the numbering is chronologically correct, and it has been mentioned in the main text that Dvořák, because he considered his first symphony irretrievably lost, invariably subtracted one from the actual complete number of his symphonies. This is understandable, and easy enough to remember. The real trouble began when the symphonies appeared in print. Simrock started to number them in order of publication, at the same time altering the opus numbers by which Dvořák had designated his works in order to make it appear that the number of symphonies tallied with their order of composition. The following table may perhaps serve to clarify the whole matter, and it should be observed that they were all first published by Simrock with the exception of Symphony No.8 in G, which was issued by Novello.

No.	Key	Composition completed	B.	Dvořák op.	First published as No.	op.	in
1	C minor	1865	9	–	–	–	–
2	B flat	1865	12	4	–	–	–
3	E flat	1873	34	10	–	posth.	1911
4	D minor	1874	41	18	–	posth.	1912
5	F	1875	54	24	3	76	1888
6	D	1880	112	58	1	60	1882
7	D minor	1885	141	70	2	70	1885
8	G	1889	163	88	4	88	1892
9	E minor	1893	178	95	5	95	1894

The second problem, however, is even more difficult. In the case of certain composers (such as Beethoven, Brahms) the opus numbers of their publication in general give a reasonably clear indication of the chronology of their works. With Mozart we owe an immense debt of gratitude to Ludwig Ritter von Köchel as a pioneer in the compilation of a thematic catalogue in chronological order. These Köchel numbers have been accepted as a standard for more than a century and are still universally in constant and customary use. When it comes to Schubert the difficulties are somewhat related to those which we encounter in the case of Dvořák, except that Schubert hardly ever (if at all) gave his works any opus numbers: all the opus numbers of Schubert's works were furnished by his publishers and are completely irrelevant as far as the time and chronology of the compositions is concerned. When Otto Erich Deutsch came out with his magnificent thematic catalogue of Schubert's works in their chronological order in 1951, only a few people championed this new system of numbering, whilst the majority sneered at it and claimed that it would never become generally accepted. Happily the scoffers were eventually proved wrong, though it took a good few years. Nowadays the antiquated opus numbers are all but forgotten, and Schubert's musical output is known generally by the Deutsch numbers (D.).

With Dvořák we have a similar problem, only still more complicated. Dvořák was in the habit of giving opus numbers to his works himself. Then, on occasion, he discarded a work as being unsatisfactory, whereby an earlier opus number became vacant which he then ascribed to a later work. Subsequently, however, in some instances he 'resuscitated' and revised such a discarded composition, and we are faced with two entirely different works bearing the same opus number from Dvořák's own hand. He was also responsible for a confusion which arose – as mentioned in the main text – from his giving certain of his works artificially low opus numbers, making them appear earlier compositions than they actually were, thereby enabling him to evade his obligations to Simrock and offer the works to other publishers who were prepared to pay a better price.

Simrock, on his part, increased the confusion still further. He gave the Dvořák works which he published whatever opus number he saw fit, at times disregarding Dvořák's wishes completely. It is only in the later years of Dvořák's life that there is some rhyme and reason, and some sort of correlation, between Dvořák's output and the printed opus numbers. It would be superfluous to go into all these matters in detail. The whole situation can perhaps be illustrated by quoting just one instance: when Dvořák had composed his Symphony No.5 in F in 1875, he numbered it op.24. Simrock published it in 1888 as No.3, op.76. Then, when it came to the Mass in D of 1887, Dvořák called it, logically and correctly, op.76 – but that was the number which had already been purloined by Fritz Simrock, so the Mass became op.86!

After all that has been said, it is obvious that the opus numbers of Dvořák's works are totally irrelevant and misleading. We are fortunate that Jarmil Burghauser has undertaken the tremendous task of compiling a Thematic Catalogue of Dvořák's works in chronological order which was published in Prague in 1960. In doing so he has done a service to Dvořák similar to that which Deutsch did to Schubert. It is natural that such an innovatory achievement cannot conquer the world in a day, especially as the Burghauser catalogue has not been sufficiently publicized, nor is it easily available. Nevertheless, it cannot be hoped too fervently that, like the Deutsch numbers, the Burghauser numbers will make their way and will eventually replace the meaningless opus numbers in designating Dvořák's individual composition. In the main it is up to music publishers, broadcasting organizations, record companies and concert-giving organizations to pave the way for the general public.

Appendix II
Chronological List of Works

The following list of Dvořák's completed and extant compositions is based on that given by Burghauser in his Thematic Catalogue. Each work is prefixed by the Burghauser (B.) number, and the opus number (if any) is given in brackets. Dates of composition refer to the completion of the original version; the dates of subsequent revisions are only listed if they deserve special mention. Titles of works in the original Czech or Latin are given in *italics*, with the English equivalents (where applicable) in Roman and in inverted commas. More detailed information about the individual works can be found in Appendix III.

Abbreviations used:

a cap.	*a cappella*
arr.	arranged, arrangement
bar.	baritone
cb.	double bass
harm.	harmonium
ma.ch.	male voice choir
mi.ch.	mixed voice choir
orch.	orchestra
org.	organ
pf.	pianoforte

quart.	quartet
rev.	revised, revision
SATB	soprano, alto, tenor, bass *soli*
sop.	soprano
str.	string(s)
timp.	timpani
tr.	trumpet
vcl.	violoncello
vl.	violin
vla.	viola

1855?	B.1	'Forget-me-not' Polka for pf.
1860	B.3	Polka for pf. in E
1861	B.7	String Quintet in A minor (op.1)
1862	B.8	String Quartet No.1 in A (op.2)
1865	B.9	Symphony No.1 in C minor
	B.10	Cello Concerto in A
	B.11	'Cypresses' for voice & pf.
	B.12	Symphony No.2 in B flat (op.4)
	B.13	Two Songs for bar. & pf.
1867	B.15	Interludes for orch.
1870	B.16	*Alfred*
	B.16a	Tragic Overture (op.1)
	B.17	String Quartet No.2 in B flat
	B.18	String Quartet No.3 in D
	B.19	String Quartet No.4 in E minor
1871	B.21	'King and Charcoal Burner' (Version I)
	B.21a	Concert Overture in F
	B.22	Potpourri from 'King and Charcoal Burner' for pf. (I)
	B.23	Five Songs for voice & pf.
	B.24	Ballad 'The Orphan' for voice & pf. (op.5)
	B.24a	'Rosmarine' for voice & pf.
1872	B.27	*Hymnus* for mi.ch. & orch. (Version I)
	B.28	Piano Quintet in A (op.5)
	B.29	Four Serbian Songs for voice & pf. (op.6)
	B.30	'Songs from the *Dvůr Králové* MS' for voice & pf. (op.7)

	B.31	Three Nocturnes for orch. (only No.2 extant)
1873	B.34	Symphony No.3 in E flat (op.10)
	B.37	String Quartet No.5 in F minor (op.9)
	B.38	Romance for vl. & pf. in F minor (op.11)
	B.39	Romance for vl. & orch. in F minor (op.11)
	B.40	String Quartet No.6 in A minor (op.12)
1874	B.41	Symphony No.4 in D minor (op.13)
	B.42	'King and Charcoal Burner' (Version II)
	B.43	Potpourri from 'King and Charcoal Burner' for pf. (II)
	B.44	Symphonic Poem (Rhapsody) in A minor (op.14)
	B.45	String Quartet No.7 in A minor (op.16)
	B.46	'The Stubborn Lovers' (op.17)
1875	B.47	*Nokturno* for str. orch. in B (op.40)
	B.48	*Nokturno* for vl. & pf. in B (op.40)
	B.49	String Quintet in G (op.77)
	B.50	Moravian Duets (I) (op.20)
	B.51	Piano Trio in B flat (op.21)
	B.52	Serenade for str. orch. in E (op.22)
	B.53	Piano Quartet in D (op.23)
	B.54	Symphony No.5 in F (op.76)
	B.55	*Vanda* (op.25)
1876	B.56	Piano Trio in G minor (op.26)
	B.57	String Quartet No.8 in E (op.80)
	B.58	Two Minuets for pf. (op.28)
	B.59	Four Songs for mi.ch. (op.29)
	B.60	Moravian Duets (II) (op.29)
	B.61	'Evening Songs' for voice & pf. (op.3, 9, 31)
	B.62	Moravian Duets (III) (op.32)
	B.63	Piano Concerto in G minor (op.33)
	B.64	*Dumka* for pf. (op.35)
	B.65	*Tema con variazioni* for pf. (op.36)
1877	B.66	Three Songs for ma. ch.
	B.67	'The Cunning Peasant' (op.37)
	B.68	*Ave Maria* for alto (bar.) & org. (op.19B)
	B.69	Moravian Duets (IV) (op.38)

B.70	Symphonic Variations for orch. (op.78)
B.71	*Stabat Mater* (op.58)
B.72	'Bouquet of Czech Folk-Songs' for ma.ch. (op.41)
B.74	Scottish Dances for pf. (op.41)
B.75	String Quartet No.9 in D minor (op.34)

1878 | B.76 | 'Bouquet of Slavonic Folk-Songs' for ma.ch. & pf. (op.43) |

B.77	Serenade for Wind Instruments in D minor (op.44)
B.78	Slavonic Dances (I) for pf. duet (op.46)
B.79	'Bagatelles' for 2 vl., vcl. & harm. (op.47)
B.80	String Sextet in A (op.48)
B.81	*Capriccio* for vl. & pf.
B.82	*Hymnus ad Laudes in festo SS. Trinitatis* for voice & org.
B.83	Slavonic Dances (I) for orch. (op.46)
B.84	Three Modern Greek Songs for voice & pf. (op.50)
B.85	*Furiants* for pf. (op.42)
B.86	Three Slavonic Rhapsodies for orch. (op.45)
B.87	Five Lithuanian Choral Songs for ma.ch. (op.27)

1879 | B.88 | 'Festival March' for orch. (op.54) |

B.89	*Mazurek* for vl. & pf. (op.49)
B.90	*Mazurek* for vl. & orch. (op.49)
B.91	The 149th Psalm for ma.ch. & orch. (Version I)
B.92	String Quartet No.10 in E flat (op.51)
B.93	Czech Suite for orch. (op.39)
B.94	Polonaise for vcl. & pf. in A
B.95	*Ave maris stella* for voice & org. (op.19B)
B.95a	*O Sanctissima* for alto, bar. & org. (op.19A)
B.97	Overture *Vanda* (op.25)
B.98	'Silhouettes' for pf. (op.8)
B.99	'Prague Waltzes' for orch.
B.100	Polonaise for orch. in E flat

1880 B.101 Eight Waltzes for pf. (op.54)
      B.102 *Hymnus* for mi.ch. & orch. (Version II)
      B.103 Eclogues for pf. (op.56)
      B.104 'Gypsy Songs' for voice & pf. (op.55)
      B.105 Two Waltzes (from B.101) for str.
      B.106 Sonata for vl. & pf. in F (op.57)
      B.107 Moravian Duets for 2 sop. & 2 altos
             (from B.60 & B.62)
      B.108 Violin Concerto in A minor
             (Final Version) (op.53)
      B.109 'Album Leaves' for pf.
      B.110 Six Piano Pieces (op.52)
      B.111 Six Mazurkas for pf. (op.56)
      B.112 Symphony No.6 in D (op.60)
      B.113 Child's Song for 2 voices
      B.114 Polka 'For Prague Students' for orch.
             (op.53/A/1)
1881 B.116 *Moderato* for pf. in A
      B.117 Ten Legends for pf. duet (op.59)
      B.118 Song 'There on Our Roof' for sop.,
             alto, & pf.
      B.119 Gallop for orch. in E (op.53/A/2)
      B.120 Quartet Movement in F
      B.121 String Quartet No.11 in C (op.61)
      B.122 Ten Legends for orch. (op.59)
      B.123 Six Songs for voice & pf.
      B.124 Four Songs for voice & pf. (op.2)
1882 B.125 *Josef Kajetán Tyl* (Overture and Incidental
             Music) (op.62)
      B.125a *Domov můj* (Overture of B.125)
      B.126 'In Nature's Realm' for mi.ch. (op.63)
      B.127 *Dimitrij* (op.64)
      B.128 Two Evening Songs for voice & orch. (op.3)
      B.128a *Otázka* ('Question') for pf.
1883 B.129 Impromptu for pf. in D minor
      B.130 Piano Trio in F minor (op.65)
      B.131 *Scherzo capriccioso* for orch. (op.66)

	B.132	Overture *Husitská* (op.67)
1884	B.133	'From the Bohemian Forest' for pf. duet (op.68)
	B.134	*Hymnus* for mi.ch. & orch. (Version III) (op.30)
	B.135	'The Spectre's Bride' (op.69)
	B.136	*Dumka* for pf. (op.12/1)
	B.137	*Furiant* for pf. (op.12/2)
	B.138	Humoresque for pf. in F sharp
	B.139	Ballad for vl. & pf. in D. minor (op.15/I)
1885	B.141	Symphony No.7 in D minor (op.70)
	B.142	Two Songs for voice & pf.
	B.143	'Hymn of the Czech Peasants' for mi.ch. & orch. (op.28)
1886	B.144	'Saint Ludmila' (op.71)
	B.145	Slavonic Dances (II) for pf. duet (op.72)
	B.146	Four Songs on Folk Poems for voice & pf. (op.73)
1887	B.147	Slavonic Dances (II) for orch. (op.72)
	B.148	Terzetto for 2 vl. & vla. in C (op.74)
	B.149	Four Miniatures for 2 vl. & vla. (op.75a)
	B.150	Four Romantic Pieces for vl. & pf. (op.75)
	B.152	'Cypresses' for str. quart. (from B.11)
	B.153	Mass in D for SATB, mi.ch. & org. (Version I) (op.86)
	B.154	The 149th Psalm for mi.ch. & orch. (Version II) (op.79)
	B.155	Piano Quintet in A (op.81)
	B.156	'Two Little Pearls' for pf.
1888	B.157	Four Songs for voice & pf. (op.82)
	B.158	'Album Leaf' for pf.
	B.159	*Jakobín* (op.84)
	B.160	Eight Love Songs for voice & pf. (op.83)
1889	B.161	Thirteen Poetic Tone Pictures for pf. (op.85)
	B.162	Piano Quartet in E flat (op.87)
	B.163	Symphony No.8 in G (op.88)

1890 B.164 Gavotte for 3 vl.
      B.165 *Requiem* (op.89)
1891 B.166 *Dumky* Trio (op.90)
      B.167 Fanfares for 4 tr. & timp.
      B.168 Overture 'In Nature's Realm' (op.91)
      B.169 Overture *Karneval* (op.92)
      B.170 Slavonic Dance for vl. & pf in E minor
             (from B.78)
      B.171 Rondo for vcl. & pf. in G minor (op.94)
      B.172 Slavonic Dance for vcl. & pf. (from B.78)
      B.173 *Klid* for vcl. & pf. (from B.133)
1892 B.174 Overture *Othello* (op.93)
      B.175 Mass in D for SATB, mi.ch. & orch.
             (Version II) (op.86)
      B.176 *Te Deum* (op.103)
      B.177 *The American Flag* (op.102)
1893 B.178 Symphony No.9 in E minor,
             'From the New World' (op.95)
      B.179 String Quartet No.12 in F (op.96)
      B.180 String Quintet in E flat (op.97)
      B.181 Rondo for vcl. & orch. in G. minor (op.94)
      B.182 *Klid* for vcl. & orch. (from B.133)
      B.183 Sonatina for vl. & pf in G (op.100)
1894 B.184 Suite for pf. in A (op.98)
      B.185 Ten Biblical Songs for voice & pf. (op.99)
      B.187 Eight Humoresques for pf. (op.101)
      B.188 Two Piano Pieces
1895 B.189 Five Biblical Songs for voice & orch.
             (from B.185)
      B.190 Suite for orch. in A (op.98b)
      B.191 Cello Concerto in B minor (op.104)
      B.192 String Quartet No.13 in G (op.106)
      B.193 String Quartet No.14 in A flat (op.105)
      B.194 Lullaby for voice & pf.
1896 B.195 'The Water Goblin' (op.107)
      B.196 'The Noon Witch' (op.108)
      B.197 'The Golden Spinning Wheel' (op.109)

	B.198	'The Wild Dove' (op.110)
1897	B.199	'Hero's Song' (op.111)
1899	B.201	'The Devil and Kate' (op.112)
1900	B.202	'Festive Ode' for mi.ch. & orch. (op.113)
	B.203	*Rusalka* (op.114)
1901	B.204	Song from 'The Smith of Lešetín'
1903	B.206	*Armida* (op.115)

Appendix III
Works in Subject Groups
(incl. Index to Compositions)

The introductory notes to Appendix II and the list of abbreviations also apply to this Appendix. In addition, the names of authors of texts are given in square brackets in Section F, Vocal Music, and the numbers in the right-hand column indicate the page(s) in the main text of the book where the most important mentions of these works occur. Where no page reference is given, these works are not specifically discussed within the text.

A. WORKS FOR THE STAGE

B. CANTATAS, MASSES, ORATORIOS

3. Serenades, Suites, Dances, Marches

4. Miscellanea

5. Works for one Solo Instrument and Orchestra

D. CHAMBER MUSIC

1. Sextets and Quintets

2. Quartets

F. VOCAL MUSIC

1. *Songs with Piano*

2. *Songs with Orchestra or Organ*

3. *Duets with Piano or Organ*

B.95a   *O Sanctissima* for alto, bar. & org.
         (op.19A), 1879
B.118   'There on Our Roof . . .' (*Na tej našej
         střeše . . .*) for sop., alto & pf., 1881

4. *Solo Voices* a cappella

B.107   Moravian Duets for 2 sop. & 2 altos,
         1880; arr. from B.60 & 62   79
B.113   'Child's Song' (*Dětská píseň*) for
         2 voices [Štěpán Bačkora], 1880

5. *Male Chorus with Piano or* a cappella

B.66   Part Songs a cap. [No. 3: A. Heyduk], 1877   86
B.72   'Bouquet of Czech folk-songs' *(Kytice
         z čes. národních písní)* a cap.
         (op.41), 1877
B.76   'Bouquet of Slavonic folk-songs' (*Z Kytice
         národních písní slovanských*) for ma.
         ch. & pf. (op.43), 1878
B.87   Five Lithuanian Part Songs a cap.
         (op.27), 1878

6. *Mixed Choruses*

B.59   Four Part Songs a cap. [Nos.1 & 2:
         A. Heyduk] (op.29), 1876
B.126   'In Nature's Realm' (*V přírodé*) a cap.
         [V.Hálek] (op.63), 1882   104
B.143   'Hymn of the Czech Peasants' (*Hymna
         českého rolnictva*) for mi.ch. & orch.
         [K. Pippich] (op.28), 1885

Appendix IV
Concordance Table

Appendix II furnishes all the information necessary to convert Burghauser into opus numbers. To facilitate conversion *from* opus *to* Burghauser numbers, the following Concordance Table may be of use. Where works which have appeared in print under one opus number but accorded various Burghauser numbers, these are separated by a comma. In the case of works which had an earlier version or were revised subsequently, such additional B. numbers are given in brackets. Also there are several opus numbers which have been variously allocated to different works on publication; these are separated by '&'.

op.			
1	B.7 & 16, 16a	11	38, 39
2	8 & 124	12	40 & 136, 137
3	61	13	41
4	12	14	44 & 42 (151)
5	24 & 28	15/I	139
6	29 & 107	16	45
7	30	17	46
8	(32) 98	18	—
9	(23) 61 & 37	19A	95a
10	34	19B	68 & 95

op. 20	B. 50	56	103 & 111
21	51	57	106
22	52	58	71
23	53	59	117, 122
24	—	60	112
25	97	61	121
26	56	62	125, 125a
27	87	63	126
28	58 & 143	64	127 (186)
29	59 & 60, 107	65	130
30	(27, 102) 134	66	131
31	61	67	132
32	62 & 107	68	133, 173, 182
33	63	69	135
34	75	70	141
35	64	71	144 (205)
36	65	72	145, 147
37	67	73	146
38	69	74	148
39	93	75	150
40	47, 48	75a	149
41	72 & 74	76	54
42	85	77	49
43	76	78	70
44	77	79	(91) 154
45	86	80	57
46	78, 83 & 170 & 172	81	155
47	79	82	157
48	80	83	160
49	89, 90	84	159 (200)
50	84	85	161
51	92	86	153 (175)
52	110	87	162
53	(96) 108 & 5, 6, 114,119	88	163
		89	165
54	88 & 101, 105	90	166
55	104	91	168

op.	92	B. 169	105	193
	93	174	106	192
	94	171, 181	107	195
	95	178	108	196
	96	179	109	197
	97	180	110	198
	98	184, 190	111	199
	99	185, 189	112	201
	100	183	113	202
	101	187	114	203
	102	177	115	206
	103	176		
	104	191		

Appendix V
Recommended Reading

As this book is primarily intended for English-speaking readers, it would be futile to give a long list of books which are only available in Czech – a language with which probably only a few of these readers are familiar. Nevertheless, it is essential to mention *the* standard work which, thus far, has not yet appeared in translation: the 4-volume work *Život a dílo Antonína Dvořáka* ('The Life and Work of Antonín Dvořák') by Otakar Šourek, who is rightly considered to be the founder of all serious Dvořák research. However, he has also written a number of works which have been published in English or German translation, and these will be dealt with later.

One reference work which is utterly indispensable to anyone concerning himself with Dvořák and his music in detail is Jarmil Burghauser's *Thematic Catalogue* (Prague 1960) which is tri-lingual (Czech/German/English). Not only does it give all relevant information about Dvořák's compositions in chronological order, but it also contains a number of facsimiles as well as a comprehensive bibliography, a survey of Dvořák's life, and much other valuable information. Burghauser is also the author of a slender booklet *Antonín Dvořák* (Prague 1966) which Supraphon has issued in a German (1966) and English (1967) translation. Brief though it is, it tells of Dvořák's life and work in a concise and comprehensive way. The same can be said of another *Antonín Dvořák* (Prague 1971) by Václav Holzknecht, published in an English translation by Orbis, although Holzknecht concentrates mainly on the music.

We must now return to Otakar Šourek. In 1929 he condensed his *magnum opus* which has been cited above into a much abbreviated *Antonín Dvořák: His Life and Work*, published in 1952 in Prague in an English translation. This book gives only a relatively short sketch of Dvořák's life and then deals in the main with his musical output. This latter aspect is greatly amplified by two further publications, *The Orchestral Works of Antonín Dvořák* and *The Chamber Music of Antonín Dvořák* (both in English translation: Prague 1956). Even though these English versions are somewhat abridged from their Czech originals, they should still prove of great help and fascinating interest to any student of Dvořák's music. In addition Šourek collated a volume entitled *Antonín Dvořák: Letters and Reminiscences* (Prague 1954) which is available in an English translation and gives much insight into the life and work of the composer. I have liberally drawn on this collection in writing the present book. Šourek also collaborated with Paul Stefan on a volume *Dvořák: Leben und Werk* (Vienna 1935) which later appeared in an English translation as: P. Stefan, *Anton Dvořák* (New York 1941).

There are, of course, many more works by Czech authors, but the above should be sufficient as a guidance. However, mention must also be made of *Antonín Dvořák: The Composer's Life and Work in Pictures* by Antonín Hořejš (Prague 1955). It has been published in a variety of translations (including English), surely the most complete pictorial survey of Dvořák's life and work in existence, and it is only marred by the fact that the pages are not numbered, and that there is no iconography or any other guide to the sources of the illustrations.

When it comes to publications in England, the earliest work that bears mention is K. Hoffmeister, *Antonín Dvořák*. Although originally issued in Czech (Prague 1924) it was the first book devoted entirely to Dvořák in an English translation printed in London (1928), but it must be admitted that it is somewhat lacking in solid substance. The first English publication which can be seriously recommended is Alec Robertson's *Dvořák* in 'The Master Musicians' series (London 1945, rev. 1964, reprinted 1969). Although by now dated, as certain facts (such as knowledge of the four early symphonies) were not yet available, it is an exceedingly well-written book, most pleasurable to read, and should be considered a 'must' for all lovers of Dvořák. Much the same can be said for *Dvořák: His Life & Music* by Gervase Hughes (London 1967) who also combines the life and the music of Antonín Dvořák into one uninterrupted and steady flow, though at times some of his statements and opinions may be contentious. In more recent times Robert Layton has written a booklet in the series of 'BBC Music Guides' (London 1978) entitled *Dvořák Symphonies and Concertos*, a most valuable addition to the Dvořák literature. Whilst it cannot replace Šourek's comprehensive volume on the orchestral works already cited, Layton's contribution will be welcomed by all those who wish for something brief, concise, and informative.

On purpose I have left John Clapham till last, not only because his two authoritative works are among the most recent, but also because he must be considered one of the leading Dvořák scholars in Britain, if not in the Western world. His first book, *Antonín Dvořák: Musician and Craftsman* (London 1966) gives a brief biographical survey but then concentrates almost exlusively on Dvořák's method of work, his style, and detailed analytical descriptions of Dvořák's musical output under well-defined headings. One of the great advantages of Clapham is that he will always be thorough in his research, meticulous when it comes to the smallest detail, and one can therefore rely on the accuracy of his information with absolute certainty. He followed up his first book with a volume entitled *Dvořák* (London 1979) which is more of a general biography without, naturally, ignoring the music. It is unnecessary to list the numerous articles which John Clapham has contributed to the musical press.

Although, to my knowledge, it is not yet available in an English translation, I feel it is imperative in this context also to list a German book on Dvořák, namely Kurt Honolka's *Dvořák in Selbstzeugnissen und Bilddokumenten* (Hamburg-Reinbek 1974) in their *RoRoRo Bildmonographien* series. This book should be a sheer delight to one and all – professional musicians and amateurs alike.

Lastly, two other works must be mentioned, though they do not relate specifically to Dvořák. The first of these is Rosa Newmarch: *The Music of Czechoslovakia* (London 1942). As can be seen by the date it is not the most modern book, and the title gives a clear indication of its scope, but it devotes fifty pages to Dvořák and, as I have said before and probably will say again, a personality such as Dvořák cannot be seen *in vacuo*, but only in correlation with the musical and other events around him. For this reason I would also strongly recommend J.F.N. Bradley's *Czechoslovakia: A Short History* (Edinburgh 1971) which is the best and most concise account I know of that most puzzling and confused history of the country in which Dvořák had his roots.

SOURCES OF ILLUSTRATIONS

Most of the illustrations were kindly put at the disposal of the author by the Antonín Dvořák Society of Prague. Where the illustrations stem from other sources, this is indicated after the caption by the letters KM (Photo Karel Mikysa), HHS (Photo Hans-Hubert Schönzeler) and PS (from Private Sources).

INDEX OF PERSONS AND PLACES in the main text